GLOBAL ISSUES SERIES

James E. Harf and B. Thomas Trout, Series Editors

POPULATION
in the
GLOBAL ARENA
actors, values, policies, and futures

PARTICIPANTS
in the Global Issues *Project*

Chadwick Alger
Ohio State University

Timothy D. King
Ohio State University

R. Trevor Bell
University of Denver

George A. Lopez
Earlham College

Arthur W. Blaser
Chapman College

Richard W. Mansbach
Rutgers University

James A. Caporaso
University of Denver

Parker G. Marden
St. Lawrence University

Kenneth A. Dahlberg
Western Michigan University

Terry L. McCoy
University of Florida

Romesh K. Diwan
Rensselaer Polytechnic Institute

Stanley J. Michalak, Jr.
Franklin & Marshall College

Raymond D. Duvall
University of Minnesota

Robert L. Paarlberg
Wellesley College

Nancy K. Hetzel
MIT

Dennis Pirages
University of Maryland

Dennis G. Hodgson
Fairfield University

Betty A. Reardon
Institute for World Order

Raymond F. Hopkins
Swarthmore College

Robert W. Rycroft
George Washington University

P. Terrence Hopmann
University of Minnesota

Donald M. Snow
University of Alabama

Barry B. Hughes
University of Denver

Marvin S. Soroos
North Carolina University

Steven I. Jackson
Cornell University

Donald A. Sylvan
Ohio State University

Robert S. Jordan
University of New Orleans

Mitchel B. Wallerstein
MIT

Roland B. Kimball
University of New Hampshire

Robert S. Walters
University of Pittsburgh

Laurie S. Wiseberg
Human Rights Internet

GLOBAL ISSUES SERIES

James E. Harf and B. Thomas Trout, Series Editors

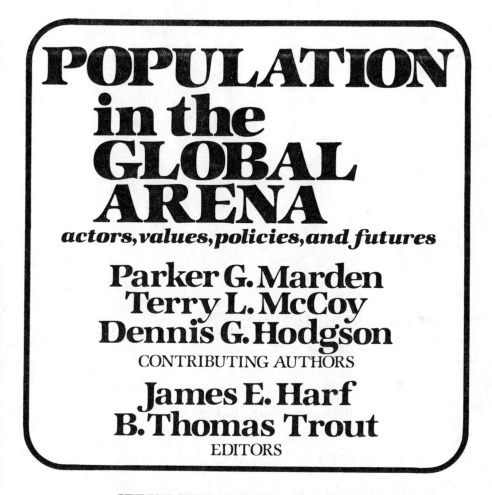

POPULATION in the GLOBAL ARENA

actors, values, policies, and futures

Parker G. Marden
Terry L. McCoy
Dennis G. Hodgson
CONTRIBUTING AUTHORS

James E. Harf
B. Thomas Trout
EDITORS

SERIES TITLES NOW AVAILABLE

Understanding Global Issues
an analysis of actors, values, policies, and futures

Energy in the Global Arena

Food in the Global Arena

Holt, Rinehart and Winston

New York   Chicago   San Francisco
Philadelphia   Montreal   Toronto   London
Sydney   Tokyo   Mexico City
Rio de Janeiro   Madrid

Library of Congress Cataloging in Publication Data

Marden, Parker G.
    Population in the global arena.

    (Global issues series)
    Includes index.
    1. Population policy. 2. Population. I. McCoy,
Terry L., 1940–   . II. Hodgson, Dennis. III. Title.
IV. Series.
HB883.5.M37   363.9   81-7211
ISBN 0-03-060061-8   AACR2

2 3 4 5   059   9 8 7 6 5 4 3 2 1

CBS COLLEGE PUBLISHING
Holt, Rinehart and Winston
The Dryden Press
Saunders College Publishing

SERIES PREFACE

This text is one in a series of volumes on contemporary issues in the global environment. The Global Issues Series, of which it is a part, is the result of a two-year project funded by the Exxon Education Foundation to develop educational resources for a number of problems arising from the shifting nature and growing interdependence of that environment. The issue areas addressed in this ongoing project include food, energy, population, environment, economic interdependence, development, arms and security, and human rights.

Each of these issues has been addressed within a systematic and integrated framework common to all. After establishing the substantive dimensions—such as the historical evolution, the structure of its global system, its basic contemporary characteristics—needed to provide the requisite foundation for inquiry, this framework is applied in separate chapters pursuing four distinct analytical perspectives: (1) Who are the *global actors* involved in the issue and what are the linkages among them? (2) What prevailing *values* are operating and how have the relevant actors responded to these values? (3) What *policies* are applied by these actors at the global level and how are these policies determined? and (4) What *futures* are represented in the values and policies of these global actors? The relationship among these perspectives and their use to link analysis of the various issues are illustrated in Figure 1. Each segment—actors, values, policies and futures—then represents a distinct analytical approach.

Thus, as an integrated structure for inquiry, the project has approached the study of global issues as an eight-by-four matrix, with the eight columns signifying eight distinct but interrelated issues and the four rows representing the four analytical perspectives or components (Figure 2). Finally, a separate volume in the series

Issues perspective	Food	Energy	Population	Environment	Economic Interdependence	Development	Arms & Security	Human Rights
Actors								
Values								
Policy								
Futures								

Figure 1

explains and rationalizes this integrating structure in relation to all of the eight issues.

In addition, differentiating this project and its product from other texts, each volume incorporates exercises that afford the student the opportunity to engage in a variety of active learning sequences—should the instructor so desire—in order to understand better the complexities of the issue.

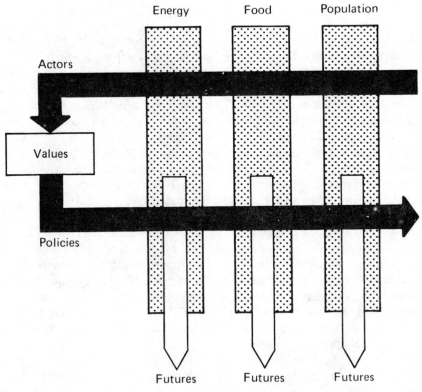

Figure 2

In realizing its goals, the project enlisted the participation of 31 prominent scholars who worked together with the project directors. These individuals contributed their substantial expertise both to specific issue areas and to the analytical development of the project as a whole.

Each volume of the series represents the specific contributions of three authors. One, the issues specialist, was responsible for the substantive introduction and summary conclusion and for supervising and coordinating the efforts of the other two authors. Those authors applied the components of the perspective framework—actors, values, policies, futures—to the issue in separate chapters. The Series editors then edited each individual volume together with the relevant issue specialist. The editors incorporated the feedback from pedagogical and substantive specialists as well as from field-testers.

The project evolved through a series of stages centered around two development workshops—the first for the "issue" and "perspective" specialists and the second for all participants—and the elaborate field-test network of the Consortium for International Studies Education. The materials developed in the workshops were produced in field-test editions which were then used across the country in a variety of instructional settings. All the volumes have therefore been revised and refined based on actual classroom experience.

We wish to acknowledge formally the financial support of the Exxon Education Foundation which provided the means to develop this project, and we wish to express our gratitude to several individuals: Roy E. Licklider, Rutgers University, who while serving with the Exxon Education Foundation encouraged us initially to pursue this venture; Richard Johnson who as our contact at the Exxon Education Foundation shepherded this project to completion; and Suzanna Easton of the Department of Education for her enthusiastic support and encouragement not only of this project but of the entire educational enterprise which it represents.

We are especially grateful to three individuals at Holt, Rinehart and Winston who have contributed greatly to the series. First we worked with Patrick Powers, who believed in this project. Marie A. Schappert brought a high professional manner and a pleasant style to her task of overseeing both the editing and marketing phases. Harriet Sigerman, as project editor, had the difficult task of translating the manuscript into print, and she did so with grace and expertise, making our lives a little easier. The same qualities were found in the typist of the final manuscript, Sheila Harvey, who delivered work of very high caliber under less than ideal schedules. Our thanks also go to Anne Sylvan and Patti Oliver for their dedicated and devoted administrative assistance. Finally, we would like to acknowledge the support of the Mershon Center and its director, Charles F. Hermann, who was forthcoming with assistance when needed.

James E. Harf
Project Director & Series Editor
The Ohio State University
Columbus, Ohio

B. Thomas Trout
Project Director & Series Editor
University of New Hampshire
Durham, New Hampshire

PREFACE

Population, once a matter only of personal or perhaps national concern, now presents itself as an issue of global significance. As Americans and as individuals who will inhabit this earth in the twenty-first century, we must make ourselves aware of the dimensions and the consequences of this fact. The issue of population, together with a number of other issues, makes us aware almost daily that we have now entered a new global era. The visual theme of this entry is that breathtaking view of our planet from space which is now taken as commonplace. That view from space portrays earth, encased in its atmospheric envelope, as an almost delicate beauty which seems to emphasize how finite is the world in which we live. Hence the variants of this theme—such as "spaceship earth" or "global village"—tell us that ours is a fragile existence with a future that is no longer limitless. We are now bound by the very dimensions that make the new view from space so startling, and so awesome.

Let us begin then to understand why it is that we consider population to be a *global issue*. Indeed, what makes an issue global? We must first think in terms of the globe itself. Global issues by definition *transcend the traditional boundaries of the nation-state* or the regional conjunction of nation-state units. We are therefore addressing issues, like population, whose impact will be felt beyond a clear confinement in terms of political or even geographic space. Thus global issues affect the judgment and actions of large segments of the world's inhabitants either directly or indirectly. Recognition of that fact, however, simply begs the question again: what are the characteristics of population which define its impact beyond such recognized accepted limits?

First, such issues are characterized by an *incapacity for autonomous decision*. No single actor, or corporate group of actors, is capable of resolving the issues associated with population—its growth, the pace of that growth, or the placement of limits on either its pace or level. It takes but a moment's reflection to recognize that the dimensions of the earth's population are the result of action by individuals and couples throughout the world. And those individuals and couples become the object of the actions, seldom concerted and often competitive, of a wide variety of governmental and nongovernmental actors at all levels. While a large number of nations may agree, as they did at the World Population Conference held at Bucharest in 1974, that population issues should be addressed at the national level, other actors such as the Catholic Church or the International Planned Parenthood Federation may not support such a position. And the various sets of actors may hold widely differing views of what action should be taken. Some may prefer a growing population in order to provide employment or military manpower; others may wish to limit population size in order to protect apparently scarce resources. The developing nations may see an obligation of the developed countries to aid in relieving the effects of population growth; the developed world, in turn, may demand population control as a prerequisite to aid. This incapacity for autonomous resolution characterizes population as a global issue. This characteristic is addressed in this volume by the *actors perspective*.

A second characteristic of global issues is that each possesses a *present imperative* which not only impels various actors to press for resolution but which encompasses the varied and often competing views as to how that resolution ought to proceed. For some time now, there has been an expression of alarm in the developed nations, particularly the United States, concerning the threat to international peace due to rapid population growth (expressed dramatically as "the population bomb"). This view has lent a growing sense of urgency to adoption of an active position advocating population control outside of the developed world. That position, however, challenges a number of countervailing values in the very target areas where the rate of population growth has been high. As noted above, national survival for some means sustained population growth. The efforts to limit such growth from already developed countries is thus seen with suspicion as a device to keep poorer nations in a state of overall dependency. Yet, again, some developing nations have perceived national survival in precisely the opposite terms and now lead the way toward population control. While an imperative is present due to population trends regardless of competing views, the outcome of those trends will depend on which values, or combination of values, will prevail. Hence, a *values perspective* provides a second analytical focus in this volume.

A third characteristic of global issues, not peculiar to such issues but nonetheless unique in the substance already defined by actors and values, is that their *resolution requires policy action*. It is evident that action—the process which combines actors with values—implies policy. The targets of such policies remain those many couples who must make individual daily choices which affect world population growth. But other actors may make choices which are more clearly policy relevant. Nation-states, for instance, may set and enforce both emigration and immigration policies which govern the movement of people and therefore population distribution. By the same token, because of the nature of the target actors, the outcome for other policy choices may be less effective and less sanguine. Policies to reduce fertility may, for example, have limited impact because there are other, competing policies active in the same arena and severe constraints upon enforcement. Couples tend to make their population decisions in private and without reference to policy pronouncements. What is more, as is the case with many other issues, policies tend to cluster and their impact must be assessed not standing alone, but in conjunction with other sets of policies. Thus, population policies may prove to be closely linked with those relating to food, to energy, to the environment, or to other perhaps more specific areas. Indeed, population policy may simply be the consequence of action taken in several of these and not in population as such. The *policies perspective* is therefore a critical nexus for understanding the interrelatedness of issues and actors affecting population in the global environment.

A final element which characterizes global issues is *their persistence*. The rhetoric surrounding such issues tends to demonstrate this element by suggesting, often with hyperbole, that human survival is at stake. Population projections have emerged with regularity from the United Nations, the World Bank, the U.S. Bureau of the Census, and other governmental and nongovernmental agencies. It is from such projections that policy prescriptions emerge and against which competing values are ranked. Projections on mortality, for example, show a continuing rate of decline based upon the diffusion of modern health procedures throughout the developing nations. The same projections for developed nations show relative little potential for change barring major medical breakthroughs. It is when such projections are linked, however, with similar analyses of fertility that a view of the prospects for global population emerges. Here the tolerances for interpretation are wider, but the results tend to point to a reasonable consensus. The developed world will tend to remain static; in the developing world the rate of population growth will begin to decline. But in the latter case the present population configuration—women now in or emerging into their childbearing years—promises a continuing high absolute growth in population. The trends and consequences of such projections are critical to understanding the global future and are, therefore, addressed in the final section on the *futures perspective.*

Three scholars are primarily responsible for this volume. Parker G. Marden, along with the Series editors, supervised it from conception to completion— selecting the other two authors, adapting the general framework to the population issue, evaluating the reviews, and editing the field-test edition and final manuscript. Mardel also contributed the first chapter, which describes the characteristics of the population issue, and the final chapter, summarizing the volume. Terry L. McCoy wrote the chapters that focus on the *actors* and *values* perspectives while Dennis G. Hodgson was responsible for the chapters on the *policies* and *futures* perspectives. The latter two also critiqued the entire volume.

A number of individuals read all or parts of this volume—and some used it in their classrooms—and contributed valuable suggestions. We wish to acknowledge Robert S. Jordan, Chadwick F. Alger, Richard W. Mansbach, and Dennis Pirages who examined, respectively, the actors, values, policies, and futures chapters;

Stanley J. Michalak, Jr. and Donald M. Snow who reviewed the entire manuscript; and Gordon L. Shull, Jonathan Flint, Rahim J. Amin, and Lester K. Beavers, who served as field-testers at their respective institutions.

James E. Harf
B. Thomas Trout

January 1982

CONTENTS

GLOBAL ISSUES SERIES

James E. Harf and B. Thomas Trout, Series Editors

POPULATION
in the
GLOBAL ARENA
actors, values, policies, and futures

chapter 1

POPULATION AS A GLOBAL ISSUE

The magnitude and pace of population growth are matters of great concern in the contemporary world. As happens with many important issues, however, as attention passes beyond that of a handful of specialists to a larger group of interested persons and decision makers, general agreement can develop, the facts can become standardized, and the details can become less important than the conclusions. There is now a form of "conventional wisdom" about population issues which consists of statements and arguments to which most persons who are concerned about global issues, at least from the vantage point of developed, Western nations, can comfortably subscribe. A measure of this development can be found in the conventions that seem to be required in introducing the problem to others.

First, discussions of population as a global issue must employ the proper imagery. They must start by stressing the finite nature of resources and the accompanying choices—"Spaceship Earth," "limits to growth," and "lifeboat ethics"—and, then, they must use the metaphors of destruction to describe the challenge of population growth to that finite world—"the Population Bomb" and "the population explosion:"

> Viewed in the long-run perspective, the growth of the earth's population has been a long, thin powder fuse that burns steadily and haltingly until it finally reaches the charge and then explodes.[1]

Second, a conventional approach must emphasize the linkages between rapid population growth and a wide-ranging set of social and environmental concerns. Brown, McGrath, and Stokes provide us with the most comprehensive list of such concerns:

> (There are) 22 dimensions of the population problem . . . Collectively, they portray the stresses and strains associated with continued population growth in a world already inhabited by four billion people.

1

literacy	declines in income
pressure on ocean fisheries	urbanization
demands for recreation	deforestation
pollution	political conflict
inflation	limits to minerals
environmental illnesses	limits to health services
hunger	water shortages
housing	unemployment
climate change	endangered species
overgrazing	energy shortages
crowding	individual freedoms[2]

Third, treatment of population *issues* must urge immediate action:

> Together with people of other nations, Americans must now decide whether there will be a future to mankind. The choice is just that simple. We must unite to solve the crises of overpopulation and pollution, abolish war, try to create a decent life for all people. If we try, perhaps there can be a very exciting, challenging, and rewarding future in the next century and beyond. But if we fail, at the very least, we can look forward to a new dark age.[3]

At a minimum, there appears to be general agreement that the solutions to various social and environmental problems that challenge humankind are exacerbated by rapid population growth. There is sufficient confidence in this assessment that metaphors have replaced hard facts in public opinion. Few persons have any sense of the size of the world's population or the rate of its growth other than the ideas that it is too large or too fast. In the increasing standardization of the discussion on population issues, many return easily to C. P. Snow's observation: "[There are] three menaces which stand in our way—H-bomb war, overpopulation, [and] the gap between the rich and poor."[4] Lord Snow's summary fits neatly for three reasons: its implications are properly awesome; it is but one step removed from the logical judgment that all three menaces are somehow interrelated; and his observation appears in an effort to bridge the "two cultures," scientific and humanistic, of which demographic matters now appear to be squarely part.

Leaving aside the evident clichés and the tired analogies, most readers interested in population matters should nonetheless not be too comfortable with these introductory remarks. Population growth does appear to present a serious challenge; such growth does seem to have great impact on society and the environment; and solutions do appear to be needed *now*. These views are the ones commonly presented by the media and in classrooms throughout the United States. They reflect the agreement of those considered to be the architects of public opinion as well as other informed persons. Unfortunately, however, reservations need to be expressed about such agreement.

First, conventional wisdom is arranged by dissenting views on the definition of the problem and explanations for it. These are based on different political approaches which are simply ignored in the process of consensus formation. Yet, when considering population as a global issue, it is imperative to recognize alternative explanations. Often, they explain the decisions reached by individuals and nations.

For example, Marxian ideology leads to conclusions about population quite different from those above. Karl Marx and Friedrich Engels considered the problems of population growth in ways that were at variance with the ideas of the social and political thinkers of their day. Inasmuch as the world is now sharply divided by commitments to such opposing philosophies, among other things, their dissent from the conventional views and their alternative explanations must be understood. They reacted specifically to the arguments of Thomas Malthus, an eighteenth-century thinker, about the dire consequences of population growth and its altering balance with available resources not only because Malthus' ideas represented the prevailing views of their time, but efforts to translate them into action directly challenged the former's conceptualization of society. They seemed to accept the explanations offered by Malthus for population growth, but they sharply disagreed with his interpretations about its consequences. For Malthus, the major result of population increase was poverty. Marx and Engels contended that poverty resulted from the organization of the system of production in a capitalist society and, thus, the problems of population growth would disappear when the workers controlled the means of production. Increases would be easily absorbed by the economy.

The Marxian approach has been translated into policy in some socialist nations. Often, the realities of population growth (and the lack of a Marxian blueprint for the period of transition from capitalism to pure socialism) have caused such policies to be modified, but usually the Marxian rhetoric is maintained even in the face of Malthusian challenges. The point here is that such alternative explanations are simply ignored or dismissed because they do not fit the conventional wisdom. As a result, many situations cannot be understood. The consistent opposition of the Soviet Union to birth control programs for Third World nations and the problems faced by China in checking a rapid population increase while maintaining an ideology that is politically consistent are but two examples.

A second problem that challenges the conventional wisdom about population issues is the fact that there is not any real agreement about solutions. One would assume that if there is consensus about the causes and consequences of population trends, it should be a reasonably short step from such understanding to agreement on potential solutions. Such is not the case. Some seek to check growth through technology by attempting to develop better contraceptives; others contend that many persons are prepared to limit their child bearing if only they can be reached with the proper message; and still others argue that the birthrate will not decline until there are major social and economic transformations.

A related difficulty about solutions is pointed up by an often told story about the student dozing in a lecture about population problems until the instructor thundered, "Do you know that somewhere in the world a woman gives birth to a child every ten seconds? What are we going to do about it?" The startled student allegedly leaped to his feet and shouted, "Find her and stop her!" This story has appeal only because it points to the dilemma faced in achieving solutions. Decisions about reproductive behavior are made not by one person (or couple), but by many thousands, indeed millions, of couples. Population trends therefore result from the aggregate of millions of individual decisions. An effective discussion of efforts to check population growth and the understanding of population dynamics must take careful note of this fact.

Finally, the conventional wisdom is challenged by the logic underlying the presentation of what many call "the population problem." Population growth is not a problem except in relationship to other variables or factors. Populations could grow indefinitely and such changes would not be perceived as a serious problem until they approached the limits of certain resources or exacerbated other difficulties. Indeed, populations have done exactly that. Their growth is perceived as a problem today not so much because growth has accelerated, although such changes in the rates are important, but because persons perceive that the "limits to growth" are being approached or even exceeded. A quick test of this assertion is to compare population growth from 1820 to 1930, in which the population doubled, with the period between 1930 and 1975, admittedly shorter, in which the population also doubled. This raises an interesting question: Does the problem occur because there are too many people or does it occur because there is too little energy, too little food, too few resources? Assuming that the proper answer is that it is both, why do most persons describe it in terms of its demographic dimensions only, that is, the population problem?

The merits of broadening our perspectives beyond the conventional wisdom can be seen by turning to the World Population Conference held under the auspices of the United Nations in Bucharest, Rumania in 1974. This major international forum for the discussion of demographic issues was designed to provide an opportunity for alerting political leaders, shapers of public opinion, and others possessing power to the problems posed by rapid population growth. It accomplished this objective, but the Conference also revealed the disagreement that existed on the very character of the problem as well as means for effecting change. Nations in the developing world questioned the right of those in more economically developed nations to set the agenda for their futures. Nations guided by a Marxist ideology challenged the definition of population growth as a problem and focused instead on the ownership of the resources available to balance some of this growth. Representatives of low-growth countries, principally in Europe, addressed a different set of challenges, and as a consequence matters of population movement between nations—legal and illegal immigration—became heated issues. The appropriateness of various measures for effecting change in fertility was also vehemently debated. The rights of women and various minority populations throughout the world were forcefully advanced. In the face of such advocacy and argument, it is difficult not to question the notions of "conventional wisdom."

One way to consider those notions is to focus upon what has become their centerpiece, "the population problem," the phrase so comfortably employed by persons who are interested in global issues. We can organize the discussion using a simple semantic distinction drawn from placing emphasis, in turn, on each of the three words that make up this phrase:

1. the population *problem*
2. *the* population problem
3. the *population* problem

Each of these separate emphases focuses our attention on a different expression of the population issue.

With the emphasis upon the word "problem," we see first the challenges of population dynamics in their usual context: What are the determinants and consequences of demographic growth? Here the issues are confronted in the form that is most usually discussed and most easily understood. Clearly, population changes, especially rapid growth, challenge and confront governments and other social institutions. Opportunities are reduced, options and alternatives are limited, and the orderly resolution of difficulties is made more difficult.

But the suggestion of the second emphasis that there is a single problem—*the* population problem—makes little sense, either as a convenient phrase or as a representation of reality. There are many variations of population dynamics, each with its own difficulties, that must be considered. Not all nations are confronted by rapid growth; some are faced with the difficulties posed by declining populations. Some European nations must import "guest workers" to provide manpower for industries and essential services. Do they share "*the* population problem" with those nations in the economically less-developed world where the problem is too many rather than too few? It would seem instead that there are many population problems.

Finally, as introduced by the third emphasis, we need to ask an important question: Is it population growth (or decline) itself that is the problem, or is it that population bumps up against something else—a limit to resources, an economic goal, a social institution? Can we talk realistically about "the *population* problem"? This simple one-dimensional conceptualization addresses only one aspect of what is almost certainly at least a two-variable issue and, more usually, a matter of many dimensions. That is, it is the population growth-limited resources problem or the population growth-environment dilemma.

Please Do Exercise 1.1: POPULATION KNOWLEDGE

THE POPULATION *PROBLEM*

We can begin our discussion of "population as a global issue" with what most persons mean when they discuss "the population problem": too many people on earth and a too rapid increase in the number added each year. The facts are not in dispute. Kingsley Davis was quite right in employing the analogy that likened demographic growth to "a long, thin powder fuse that burns steadily and haltingly until it finally reaches the charge and explodes."[5]

To understand the current situation, which is characterized by rapid increases in population, it is necessary to understand the history of population trends as Davis suggests. Rapid growth is a comparatively recent phenomenon. Figure 1.1 presents 8,000 years of demographic history and shows that populations have been virtually stable or growing very slightly for most of human history. Indeed, for only the past two or three centuries has the principal demographic or societal issue been anything other than survival. For most of our ancestors, life was hard, often nasty, and very short. There was high fertility (births) in most groups, when it was not checked by low fecundity (fecundity is simply the ability to have children) due to disease or poor nutrition, but this was usually balanced by high mortality (deaths). For most of human history, it was seldom the case that one in ten persons would live past forty, while infancy and childhood were especially risky periods. Often, societies were in clear danger of extinction because death rates could exceed their birthrates for extended periods. Thus, the population problem throughout most of history was how to prevent extinction of the human race. Obviously, barring a worldwide natural or human catastrophe, this historical problem has been eliminated.

This pattern is important to note. Not only does it put the current problems of demographic growth into a historical perspective, but it suggests that the cause of rapid increases in population in recent years is not a sudden enthusiasm for more children, but an improvement in the conditions that traditionally have caused high mortality. Thus as Figure 1.1 shows, demographic history can be divided into two major periods: (1) a time of long, slow growth (and occasional declines) which extended from about 8000 B.C. (and the beginnings of the Agricultural Revolution) until approximately A.D. 1650 and (2) a period of rapid, dramatic growth since

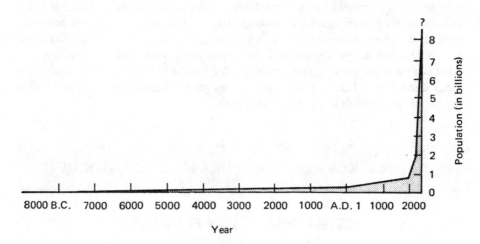

Figure 1.1

WORLD POPULATION GROWTH

1650. It is not happenstance that the dividing line of 1650 also marks the beginning of the modern era. In the first period of some 9,600 years, the population increased from some eight million to 500 million in 1650. Between 1650 and the present, the population has increased from 500 million to more than 4 billion. And it is projected that by the year 2000 there will be 6.2 billion people throughout the world. One way to appreciate this dramatic difference in such abstract numbers is to reduce the time frame to something that is more manageable. Between 8000 B.C. and 1650, an average of only 50,000 persons was being added annually to the world's population each year. At present, this number is added every six hours! The increase is about 80,000,000 persons annually!

This substantial acceleration in demographic growth is reflected in a different way in Table 1.1. While it took many thousands of years for the size of the world's population to reach one billion people—around 1820 A.D.—it required only 110 years (1820–1930) to add the next billion and 25 years (1930–1965) to add the third billion. The fourth billion was added in only ten more years, by 1975, and at the present rate of increase, an additional billion is added approximately every ten years. Not only do such figures reveal the magnitude and velocity of population growth in the past three centuries, and the present one in particular, but they suggest

Table 1.1
Growth of the World's Population

Year	Population	Percent Increase Per Year since the Previous Date	Years to Double since the Previous Date
10,000 B.C.	1–10 million	a	b
5000 B.C.	5–20 million	a	b
0	200 million	a	b
A.D. 1300	400 million	a	b
1650	.5 billion	.1	1,000
1700	.6 billion	.2	300
1750	.7 billion	.3	230
1800	.9 billion	.4	180
1850	1.2 billion	.5	140
1900	1.6 billion	.6	120
1950	2.4 billion	.8	90
1970	3.6 billion	2.1	33
1975	4.0 billion	2.1	33

[a] Smaller than .05 percent.
[b] A very large number of years.

All figures are rounded to avoid a false impression of accuracy. Even today world population totals are not highly accurate; early figures are best described as informed guesses. However, the overall import of the table is factually substantiated.

*A.M. Carr-Saunders, *World Population*, The Clarendon Press, Oxford, 1946, p. 42: United Nations, *Demographic Yearbook*, New York, various dates; and Bernard Berelson *et al.*, "World Population: Status Report 1974," *Reports on Population: Family Planning*. No. 15. January 1974, p. 3.

Source: Thomlinson, 1976: 18.

the importance of understanding the Malthusian logic that underlies them. Malthus argued that population, if unchecked, has the capacity to increase geometrically: 1, 2, 4, 8, 16, 32, 64, 128, and so on, while resources, at best, cannot grow as rapidly. In advancing this argument, he was reflecting the possibilities for exponential growth that exist in human populations. For example, if four couples each have three children (12), and each of them marries one of their number and has three children, then they will have produced a second generation of 18 (that is, six couples with three children each). Repeated twice more, the third generation will total 27, the fourth will be around 40. To gain some appreciation of the problems of managing demographic growth, place the original four couples in a house with four apartments or on four adjacent farms. When one recognizes that generations overlap—here nearly all of the last three generations, or 85 people (18 + 27 + 40), are likely to be alive at the same time—the difficulties are underscored. The need for new housing or more land becomes increasingly acute, and represents a whole range of problems that must be considered when we move from an abstract example to the real world.

Even as these theoretical calculations are worked out in reality, there are two additional factors that do not bode well. First, the assumption of three children is simply too low to represent the fertility of many nations of the world. In India, for example, the number of children per woman exceeds 6.0; in Mexico, it is as high as 6.5; and in Algeria, it is nearly 7, more than 5 of whom will survive to adulthood and their own reproductive activity. In these nations each generation is nearly 80 percent larger than the one before it. Other economically less-developed nations have similar patterns and because of the size of their populations—the high-growth nations include about three-fourths of the world's population—the matter of momentum is especially acute. Second, mortality (the death rate or the number of deaths per 1,000 population in a given year), especially that of young children, has been declining throughout the world. This decline contributes to population growth in several ways. Obviously, the numbers removed from the population by death are reduced, but fertility is also enhanced. More persons live to reach reproductive age and, concomitantly, impairments to fecundity are reduced by the same factors that caused mortality to decline. In addition, traditional fertility patterns have often been premised upon the anticipation of high mortality among the offspring. It takes at least one generation to recognize the increased chances for survivorship and adjust to it. In the meantime, the momentum of population growth is in full swing.

The implications of these matters for future population growth are substantial. Even the most conservative estimates for such growth and the most optimistic of analysts anticipate substantial increases in the world's population. As detailed above, there is a built-in momentum to current demographic patterns. Although there have been significant reductions in the fertility of some nations, these successes need to be judged against the magnitude of the situation. If, for example, the fertility of women in India or Mexico, reflected by the average number of children per woman, could be cut in half, the situation would be dramatically improved. But an average of three children would still bring these women only to the fertility patterns reflected in the theoretical example offered initially. The population would still be growing exponentially! It is little wonder, then, that population growth is viewed as a significant global issue. Population problems have a comparatively short history as a major concern, but it does not appear as if they will disappear in the immediate future.

Please Do Exercise 1.2: A DEMOGRAPHIC RIDDLE

The Demographic Transition

Why have populations grown so rapidly in such a short time? A useful construct by which to explain the dynamics of population change that underlie these trends is the model of *the demographic transition*. There is a debate about the theoretical implications of this theory or model. The major problem centers on its predictive value and many argue that it fails to distinguish between description and causal explanation.[6] But if we treat it as a model that *describes* what has happened to various populations and leave its more theoretical possibilities (and difficulties) to others, it allows us to understand the mechanisms for demographic growth in the past and present and the potentialities for future changes.

The transition model is premised on the fact that there are only three variables that can cause populations to change: fertility, mortality, and migration. Fertility (births) and in-migration add persons to a population; mortality (deaths) and out-migration remove persons from that population. Populations grow or decrease through various combinations of these variables and the' possibilities are conveniently summarized in this demographic equation:

$$P^{now} = P^{then} + \text{Births} - \text{Deaths} \pm (\text{In-Migration} - \text{Out-Migration})$$

To illustrate, a population of 100 in 1975 in which there were 17 births and 8 deaths and a net migration of 3 (10 moving in and 7 moving out) in a five-year period would have a population of 112 in 1980.

In the case of the world and most of its nations, the role of migration as a factor in changing the size of the total population can be ignored when the demographic transition is considered (although it will remain as an important factor in determining the distribution of that population) and the model involves a specification of changing relationships of the two biosocial variables, mortality and fertility, over time. Through it, we can quickly understand why populations suddenly began to grow.

Figure 1.2 portrays the changing patterns of fertility and mortality that characterize the demographic transition. There are three major periods reflected in the model. Two periods in which birthrates and death rates are in balance and do not change greatly (A and C) are separated by a time of imbalance in which there is rapid growth (B). It is this period of transition with its dramatic increase in population that provides the name for the model.

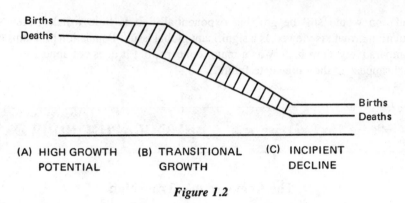

Figure 1.2

THE MODEL OF THE DEMOGRAPHIC TRANSITION

The first period (A) is a time of *high growth potential*. The birthrates and death rates are both high, but they exist in relative balance. Living conditions are harsh and the life spans of people are short. Populations do not grow very much and fertility must be purposely high because anything lower would challenge the very survival of the group.

The second period (B), *transitional growth,* is a time in which changes begin to occur. The two vital processes, mortality and fertility, begin to diverge as the death rates decline, but birthrates remain high for a number of years before they also begin to decrease. The balance between the two rates is upset and the resulting disequilibrium leads to considerable population growth. Simply put, many more persons are being added to the population through the continued high rates of fertility than are being removed through death because of declining mortality. The result is the population explosion reflected in the data presented above. Its pattern, high fertility and low mortality, presently characterizes most of the economically less-developed nations.

Eventually, fertility declines and strikes a new balance with mortality. Both the birth and death rates are now low. Generally, this pattern characterizes the demographic situation of most economically developed nations and because of the new balance between the two vital processes, populations grow relatively slowly, if at all. This period (C) is one of *incipient decline*.

The reasons for these changes are complicated but, essentially, both are related to a process of social and economic transformation that began with the modern era. As a result, the year 1650 as the demarcation point for such changes divides two distinctive demographic patterns as reflected here. Mortality declines because of better agriculture and better transportation, improved sanitation, the development of asepsis and antisepsis, a rising standard of living, and similar factors. There were few impediments to the adoption of such factors since they were fully compatible with the prevailing culture and social structure. Nearly anything that would prolong life was quite acceptable to all involved.

Human fertility, however, is tied up in a set of values and attitudes that have favored large families with many children and which have been nurtured for many centuries to avoid the demise of the society. Such norms change slowly and, in part, this results from the fact that the realization that mortality is declining can only be gradual. Eventually, in those nations that have moved to the period of incipient decline (C), fertility responds to the same processes of change that cause mortality to decline, although here the operative factors center on a decreasing value of large families in urban-industrial settings where children are more likely to be economic liabilities than assets. But the lag between declines in mortality and fertility, often lasting two or three generations, is a period of great growth.

Thus, there has been a dramatic transformation in population growth. As the model of the demographic transition suggests, the change has occurred not because there were significant changes in fertility, but because the traditional check on growth—high mortality—was rendered ineffective by a social and economic transformation.

Comparative Patterns of Population Growth

One of the major advantages of the transition model is the opportunity it offers to position the various nations with respect to their current demographic situation and potential for future growth. This is important because a major feature of the present situation is the sharp difference between nations with respect to fertility and mortality and the gap between these two variables. If population is a global issue, then these differences, especially those that distinguish the economically developing nations from those who are economically more developed, are principal reasons.

The possibilities in this regard are reflected in Figure 1.3. The "classic" pattern of the demographic transition is reflected in the data on fertility and mortality for Sweden, a now developed nation for which reasonably complete data have been available for 150 years. In 1820, there was a close balance between the Swedish birth and death rates, but both rates were high (viz. Period A in the demographic transition model). In the 1830s the number of deaths even exceeded births for a time and, exclusive of the possible effects of migration, Sweden faced population decline. Over time, both rates declined, but mortality fell more rapidly than fertility. A period of transitional growth extended for more than eighty years (Period B). Eventually, a new balance of low birth and death rates was struck, although increase in fertility or "the baby boom" after World War II suggests the fluctuations that are always possible in growth rates (Period C).

The patterns for Sweden can be contrasted with those for two economically less-developed nations: Sri Lanka (formerly Ceylon) and Mexico. The information for few nations is available for as long a period as Sweden and the limitations are especially acute for those of the developing world. But the patterns of the transition are clear. Both developing nations are in periods of rapid transitional growth (Period B). At present, for example, the birth and death rates for Mexico are 42 and 11 per 1,000, respectively, producing a rate of natural increase of 3.3 percent annually (that is, 36 per 1,000). Translated into actual population figures, this means that 11,655,000 of its estimated population of 71,800,000 in 1980, or one-sixth of the total, were added in the last five years (1975–1980). Stated another way, one of every six Mexicans now alive was born in the last five years. The figures for Sri

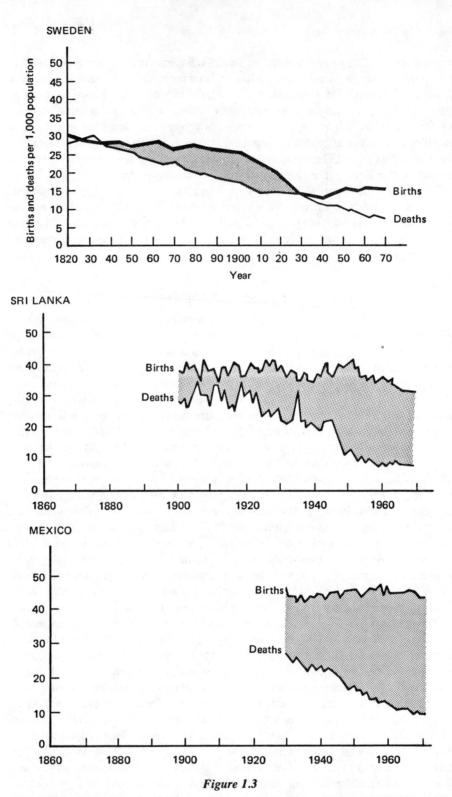

Figure 1.3

THE DEMOGRAPHIC TRANSITION IN SWEDEN, SRI LANKA (CEYLON), AND MEXICO

Lanka, a smaller nation in South Asia, are also dramatic, and these two examples are representative of nations throughout the developing world. Comparable rates in 1980 for Sweden, as a representative of nations throughout the economically developed world, were 11 births and 9 deaths per 1,000 or a rate of natural increase that is nearly in balance. In the five years (1975—1980) in which Mexico was increasing its population by nearly 20 percent, Sweden added 105,000 or just 1.3 percent.

It is important to note some of the differences between the Swedish experience and the present vital rates for the two developing nations presented in Figure 1.3, Mexico and Sri Lanka, not to mention the variations between these two nations which, hopefully, suggest both the continuities and differences that exist throughout the countries of the developing world. These countries, like most of their economically developing counterparts, have much higher birthrates than did Sweden at comparable levels of mortality. In 1940, for example, as Mexico's mortality really began to decline, its death rates became approximately comparable with Sweden's mortality a century earlier. At the same time, Mexico's birthrate was about 25 percent higher than the Swedish rate had been at any point in the 160 years for which good records are available. Thus, the transitional growth that these differentials reflect is dramatically higher.

The presentation in Figure 1.3 also does not fully reveal another major difference between the demographic transition that took place in Sweden (and other developed nations) and the present patterns of population growth in the economically less-developed nations. Sweden took more than a century to complete its transition from the "old" pattern of high, but balanced vital rates to the "new" balance of low rates of fertility and mortality. The trend was relatively slow and gradual and the various social institutions that needed to adjust to such changes had a comparatively easy task. For most developing nations, however, the demographic changes are much more dramatic and stressful. The techniques of mortality control are easily transported from one nation to another both because of their low cost and relatively easy application (for example, malaria control, smallpox prevention) and their compatibility with societal norms and values. The decline in death rates in these nations has been very abrupt as a result of the transference of such technology after World War II.

Fertility control is quite another matter. Although the technology of birth limitation is relatively simple and transferable, its acceptance is far more problematic. High fertility is deeply imbedded in the various cultures and it is well supported by their institutional structure. In Sweden and the other nations that have passed through an economic and social transformation, the values gradually changed and the pace of declining mortality was sufficiently slow so that the amount of transitional growth was never overwhelming. Today, if the goal for developing nations is to complete a transition to a state of incipient decline—a goal on which there may not be consensus—then the choice is between waiting patiently for a transformation in values and behavior concerning fertility (a pattern that was acceptable in the demographic history of developed nations) and attempting to force the issue in some way. Much of the debate over population policies for economically less-developed nations centers on this issue of pacing and patience. A number of questions are implicit within it: Will these nations follow the pattern of more-developed nations (that is, is the transition model applicable?)? How much time will the transformation require? How much time do we have? How fair is it for nations that underwent a demographic transition in a relatively leisurely fashion to force a new schedule on their less-developed counterparts? These questions lie at the heart of the debate over population policies.

One thing is not at issue, however. It is clear that there are major differences between nations with respect to both their present patterns of population increase and their potential for continued growth. Figure 1.4 arranges the various regions of the world with respect to their annual rates of population increase. The regions, in

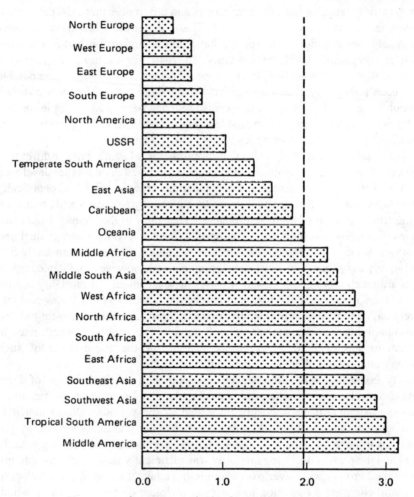

Average annual rate of population growth in 1975 (percent)

Figure 1.4

REGIONAL DIFFERENCES IN POPULATION GROWTH

The vertical broken line represents the *world's* average rate of growth in 1975.
Source: Weeks, 1978: 46. (Data from Population Reference Bureau)

turn, arrange themselves almost perfectly in the order of the degree of economic development that characterized them. The nations of Europe, North America, and the U.S.S.R. head the list with the lowest rates and the developing nations follow. The dimensions of the problem of potential growth are quickly revealed by noting that the greatest proportion of the world's population lives in those nations that are less-developed and which have the highest rates of natural increase. The economically developed, low-growth regions presently represent only one-fourth of the world's population and the continued growth of the developing regions widens this gap every day!

Despite the clear dichotomy that exists between the regions that are principally composed of nations that are economically less-developed and those which are economically more advanced, a warning against sweeping generalizations needs to be sounded. The growth rates for South Korea, Hong Kong, Taiwan (Republic of China), and Japan are significantly lower than those of other Asian nations. The nations of temperate South America—Argentina, Chile, and Uruguay—have growth rates that are about one-half of those of tropical South America or Middle America. All Latin American nations are not alike in their demographic patterns, as well as the social, political, and economic conditions that these reflect, despite common (and obviously mistaken) perceptions of their neighbors to the north.

In summary, there are three important facts that must be drawn from this review of demographic history if population problems are to be appreciated as a global issue: (1) the population of the world is growing rapidly; (2) even if programs to control human fertility are immediately successful, there is a momentum to this growth that will cause it to continue; and (3) the magnitude of the increases is disproportionately distributed with the less-developed nations becoming a significantly larger proportion of the world's total population.

Clearly, then, there is a "population *problem*." To appreciate it fully, we need to consider it in both absolute, or total, and relative terms. Consider those nations that face rapid population growth. Although the difficulties that they encounter as a result will vary from one nation to another because of the particular combinations of history, resources, culture, national psychology, and similar attributes that distinguish them, all will find certain courses of action eliminated and choices reduced. As population growth creates heightened demand for a particular resource, for example, limited funds may need to be diverted to new domestic investment or purchases abroad. Either alternative will place limits on what else can be done. This is the common denominator of rapid population growth. Individual nations, and when taken together, the world, face sharply diminishing choices in the face of the "population explosion."

But the fact that the pace and magnitude of population growth vary significantly among nations, with the economically less-developed nations facing the greatest challenges and the most limited options, demands that the *relative* dimensions of the problem also be understood. The political, social, and economic volatility of such developments is obvious. The relationships between nations, or between convenient groupings, such as "developed" and "developing," are conditioned by differential patterns of growth. Since they divide "have-not" nations from their more affluent counterparts, they separate the nations facing the greatest challenges from those who have often been quick to offer advice along with more material forms of aid. Further, they are conditioned by the fact that economic growth of the now-developed nations has been based in large part on the resources extracted from colonies and other areas that are now independent nations grappling with the difficulties posed by dramatic increases in their populations. At present, there are dramatic disparities in consumption in the two sectors of the world. The economically developed nations, taken together, consume 60 to 70 percent of the world's resources, yet they contain only one-third of the total population. In an era of rising national self-awareness and self-assertion, following this history of diverting resources to the use of the now-developed nations, the growing gap between rich and poor nations influences what can be done, by whom, and when. "Solutions" to population problems are matters of politics and social psychology as well as demography.

THE POPULATION PROBLEM

To this point, the discussion has outlined the parameters of what is popularly called the population problem. Just as no one mistakes "*the* pill" for aspirin, the phrase "population problem" has come to signify the challenge posed by demographic growth and the large numbers being added to various populations of the world. In this sense, the discussion above is reasonably complete and one with which those with a general awareness of population issues can be comfortable.

But there are other dimensions to population dynamics that are of equal importance in many instances. Concern for population size and its growth to the exclusion of other issues is problematic for three reasons. First, it ignores the fact that population as an issue is more than a matter of demographic concern, but involves many nondemographic issues as well, such as social or economic aspects. This matter will be explored in the next section. Second, the particular difficulties faced by some nations and specific regions within most nations often differ from more general patterns, but pose very real demographic challenges to them. Some areas may be growing just as other areas are declining and each set has appropriately different needs. Third, when discussions of the population problem end with a consideration of numbers, other important and related demographic variables are overlooked. The composition and distribution of population, for example, can exacerbate the difficulties presented by high rates of growth and pose real dilemmas for policymakers. The problems of allocating limited resources between growing rural and urban populations, for example, challenge many governments. Each may have quite different needs and pose quite different political challenges.

The "Optimum" Population

Efforts to estimate the carrying capacity of the earth (or individual nations) or the optimum (proper or "correct") population illustrate some of these difficulties. For many years, persons have attempted to determine how many persons could be sustained by the earth's resources. In a phrase, how many can "Spaceship Earth" carry? Malthus, for example, struggled with this issue when he charted the relationship between the *arithmetic* growth of resources (1, 2, 3, 4, 5, 6, 7, 8, 9) and the *geometric* growth of population (1, 2, 4, 8, 16, 32, 64, 128, 256). To him, the crisis would occur when demographic growth outstripped the resources that were available. Other more exacting efforts to estimate the extent of available resources have also been made in recent years. But, like the efforts undertaken by Malthus, these are often flawed because they cannot fully anticipate changes in technology, the capacity to utilize resources of varying quality, social and political organization, and the values and perceptions of populations. Many efforts to estimate the balance that exists (or will exist) between population and resources are examples of "one-dimensional ecology" in that these other factors are not considered. Many recent efforts to estimate the earth's carrying capacity, culminating in such recent concepts as "Spaceship Earth" and "lifeboat ethics" and proposals for "triage" for nations of the economically less-developed world, are examples. Although the pessimism of such efforts may be correctly placed, the supporting evidence needs to be assembled and carefully evaluated. Thus, it is important to place the "population crisis" in a nondemographic context and explore the various social and cultural facts that may permit adjustments to certain challenges. We shall return to this point below.

A set of variations on attempts to establish the carrying capacity of the earth involves the effort to identify "optimum populations." Here, the concern is less a matter of establishing the limits of growth than one of determining an ideal population for specified purposes. While questions of "carrying capacity" are usually restricted to estimates of the quantity, quality, and accessibility of resources, discussions of the optimum size and character of a specific population are broader. This leads immediately to the question that is always raised: "Optimum for what?"

This question anticipates the major dilemma (and debate) faced in nations as they cope with the various results of population dynamics. The population characteristics which may be suitable for one purpose may be quite problematic for another. For example, a nation may view a large population, especially of young adults, as having certain military and economic advantages and, as a consequence, their policies may be deliberately pronatalist (that is, favoring population growth). The strain that continued growth may then place on various institutions—education and health services being prime examples—suggests that others may define optimum size and rates of growth differently. This dilemma is underscored by the contradictions that exist in national policies concerning population. For example, most economically developed nations have a set of population policies that are contradictory in being both pronatalist and antinatalist (that is, supporting population limitation). Income tax deductions and family allowances that "reward" high fertility often exist side by side with incentives and programs to reduce family size. Similar contradictions exist in the economically less-developed nations, but here the contradictions are quickly pointed out by advocates for reduced fertility who see pronatalist policies as illogical. The debate soon becomes one of who has the right to establish the agenda for discussion. It is important not to lose sight of the fact that the question "optimum for what?" can be answered in different ways.

This situation can also be clearly seen within nations as local areas struggle with quite different population issues. For example, the problems of declining school enrollments in the United States, reflecting decreases in fertility in recent years, pose significant challenges for school systems at all levels. But there is considerable variability in the way in which this challenge manifests itself. Many school districts are facing the problems of retrenchment, but others must meet the demands of expanding enrollment. For some of these areas, the influx of new students because of migration requires sensitivity to students from different cultural and language backgrounds. What, then, is *the* population problem? Obviously, the variability of the demographic circumstances faced by various civil divisions within nations— communities, states, and regions—confronts the notion that population growth is a single challenge. The fact that many areas are facing declining enrollments where the problems were those of rapid growth less than a generation earlier suggests that the challenges are not identical over time either.

A Wider Range of Issues

Possibly the greatest difficulty in restricting attention to "*the* population problem" is that it focuses upon a narrow range of demographic concerns. As presented, it is a matter of increased size of populations produced by a combination of high fertility and declining mortality. But as Figure 1.5 suggests, population analysis involves other important variables and a wide range of possible combinations among them.

As a discipline, demography focuses upon only six basic variables. The interrelationships among them and consideration of their determinants and consequences, however, can guarantee lifetimes of work. There are the three *process* variables already mentioned—fertility, mortality, and migration. They in turn interact to produce changes in populations which can be specified as matters of three *structural* variables: size, composition, and distribution. These, in their turn, can again influence the three processes.

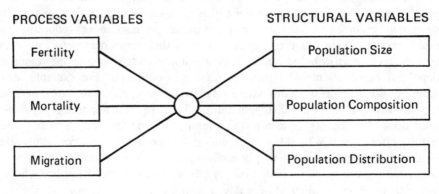

Figure 1.5

THE POPULATION VARIABLES

The demographic equation, $P_{now} = P_{then} + Births - Deaths \pm Migration$, suggests how the three demographic processes combine, in varying contributions, to produce a population of a new size. But they also interact to change the *composition* and *distribution* of the population as well. For example, high fertility adds large numbers of younger persons to a population, causing its average age to be lowered. The figures presented earlier for Mexico are illustrative since the one-sixth of its 1980 population that was added since 1975 is still five years of age or younger. Young populations require quite different societal responses than do older ones. Similarly, fertility and mortality rates may vary between urban and rural areas, causing one to grow more rapidly than the other, quite apart from the contribution of migration. But migration can add dimensions of its own since it is usually young adults, with the greatest potential for childbearing, who are in motion. Their reproductive decisions can be very influential. Since movement is predominantly from rural areas to large urban centers, the question of whether these migrants will maintain the usual rural pattern of large families in the city or adopt a smaller family ideal is an important one. Thus, the composition and distribution of population "feedback" on the demographic processes, producing new patterns of fertility, mortality, and migration.

Full exploration of these six variables—three process and three structural—of their interaction, and of the various determinants and consequences is beyond the scope of the present enterprise. The point here is to emphasize that talk of "*the* population problem," however troubling it may be, narrows the discussion to one set of relationships between variables. It denies attention to other demographic problems that can be equally worrisome. For some nations, the central population issues may be ones that result from a quite different combination of variables. For others in which the rate of population growth and increasing size are the major concerns, a restriction of attention to these matters may overlook the importance of other factors, especially the population's composition and distribution.

Declining Population. For most of the world's nations, the population is growing rapidly. For some, however, populations are relatively stable with very slow rates of population growth and, for a few, the balance between fertility and mortality is such that there are negative rates of natural increase. In 1980, for example, the estimated growth rate for West Germany was −0.3 percent per annum (with a birth-rate of about 9 per 1,000 and a death rate of 12 per 1,000). Astute students of language will note the contradiction in speaking of negative growth—a term conditioned by years, indeed centuries, of thinking only about population increases with an accompanying attitude toward planning. The result in West Germany is a net loss of population—an estimated 932,000 between 1975 and 1980, an aging population with increasing needs for medical and social services, and an economy that must import workers from abroad if it is to continue to grow and prosper.

The problems of West Germany, in various forms, are found throughout the economically developed nations. Economies that have been based upon growth and expansion for their vitality now face manpower shortages. Social welfare systems, including Social Security and other retirement programs, now find that the proportion of persons making claims against them, especially the aged, are more numerous than in days past when the funding mechanisms were designed. While absolute declines in populations are found only in a few nations as yet, decreases in fertility and the resulting shifts in age structure are challenging the economic, social, and political institutions of many developed nations. For many nations— France, Germany, Austria, Hungary, and others—this situation has become a matter of great national concern. In the United States, discussions are more muted, but the concern for population growth is being replaced by considerations of ways to stimulate economic growth and social progress without an expanding population. To these nations, then, what is *the* population problem? While their futures are closely entwined with those of developing nations where rapid growth is a major concern, the problems that they immediately confront are derived from different demographic realities. The conceptualization of *the* population problem as a concern for rapid growth does not fit these realities.

Immigration. The difficulties faced by Eastern and Western European nations in coping with declining growth rates (or even negative rates) serve to point to the importance of migration, the third process variable, which is overlooked in standard constructions of *the* population problem. A number of these nations have been required to import persons to fill the openings in their labor forces. These immigrants, euphemistically called "guest workers," provide many of the non-skilled, but basic services essential to the economy of the ordinary day-to-day operations of a society. These workers are not permanent residents, a relationship often reinforced by carefully contrived legal mechanisms, but their presence is very important. In England and Germany, one of every seven manual workers is a migrant; in France, Switzerland, and Belgium, the number is one of every four.[7]

The guest workers are very controversial in most of their European settings. Most are men who work to support families at home which they may visit once a year. They are predominantly from developing nations, often from the former colonies of the host country, and they represent large, ghettoized populations in many major cities. Their presence can challenge the definition of who is French, or German, or Swiss, and the clash of cultures and languages is a major issue. But the economies of Europe require their presence. So, for the nations that depend upon them, migration is an important demographic process. In large part, its importance has been heightened by declining rates of natural increase.

The situation of the guest workers in Europe underscores another connection between economically developed and the less-developed nations. It is in the economies of the latter nations with labor forces that are unable to absorb willing workers that the manpower for European manufacturing and service industries is found. Exchanges between these two sets of nations are found throughout the world. The United States, for example, is a nation bordered immediately on the south by Mexico, which has a ready reserve of unemployed and underemployed workers because of high rates of population growth. Many come north to explore what are their only reasonable prospects for employment. Controversy over this stream of "nondocumented" or "illegal" immigrants ebbs and flows with the fortunes of the American economy. The stream itself changes with the state of the Mexican economy. Similar situations are found when considering immigrants, including political refugees from Cuba, Vietnam, Cambodia, Haiti, Colombia, and other developing nations. The matter is especially perplexing in a nation that considers immigration as an important part of its heritage and the process of nation building.

But the problem of accommodating migrants or blocking their movement is not limited to a flow between economically less-developed nations and those of Europe and North America. The booming economies of Saudi Arabia and the oil-rich emirates of the Persian Gulf are manned by migrants from Africa and Asia; the presence of Salvadorans in Honduras provoked a major military confrontation in the 1960s; Venezuela and Colombia have major disputes over population movements between the two nations; and the shifting of populations between African nations, both as matters of economic necessity and political changes, is an important aspect in the understanding of current events in that region. So, despite its absence from standard formulations of "*the* population problem," migration requires appropriate attention as an issue.

Population Composition. In the present context, population composition receives particular attention because it is so closely related to the problem posed by rapid increases in population size. It requires particular emphasis in considering population as a global issue.

The same gaps between fertility and mortality that cause population growth also produce a composition of a population that is distinctive and challenging. High-growth countries have dramatically younger age structures than do those of low growth, and the stresses that these children place on the institutions of society, especially those involved in education, accentuate the dilemmas posed by rapid growth.

Figure 1.6 suggests the shape that the age-sex structure of a population can take under three separate assumptions about fertility and growth if these were maintained over an extended period of time. In all three cases, the rates of mortality and migration have been held constant, although obviously these variables can influence the structure of a population as well. Migration, in particular, can change the shape almost overnight since migrants often share certain characteristics (for example, young adults, 18−30, in search of employment). Here, low fertility produces a population distribution that is almost rectangular in shape since there are nearly the same percentage of persons at each age. The shape resulting from high fertility is quite different, roughly pyramidal, with many more younger persons in the population.

Figure 1.7 provides the age-sex structures for Mexico, Sweden, and the United States as a reasonable approximation of the contrast between economically developing and more-developed nations. With its recent history of rapid growth, Mexico (Figure 1.7A) has a pyramidal structure. In fact, nearly one-half of its total population is under the age of 15. The shape of the population structure for Sweden (1.7B) as a low-fertility nation is almost rectangular. Here, the proportion of young

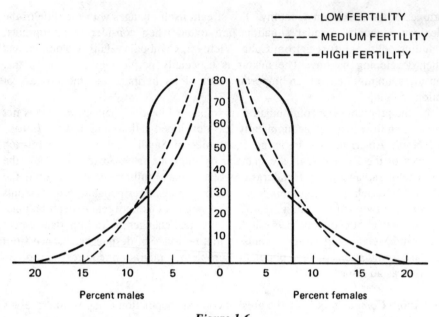

Figure 1.6

**EFFECTS OF DIFFERENT LEVELS OF FERTILITY ON THE AGE/SEX
DISTRIBUTION (HYPOTHETICAL)**

Source: Weeks, 1978: 161.

persons, 0–14, is less than 23 percent—about one-half of Mexico's figure. The profile for the United States (1.7C) is obviously much closer to the Swedish case, although it is instructive to consider the unevenness in the various five-year age groupings. Here, the demographic fluctuations over time, especially in fertility, are portrayed and the figure reflects the so-called baby boom (ages 5–29 in 1970) and suggests how it was a deviation from a pattern of low fertility which is beginning to reassert itself in the 1960s as reflected in the age group 0–4.

The importance of age composition as a crucial variable comparable to population size can be derived from these graphic presentations. High-fertility populations are not the only ones that have a disproportionately large number of young persons. Mexico is not atypical in having nearly one-half of its population under the age of 15. The consequences of this pattern are quite serious. The interrelationships between composition and general population growth can be seen simply by looking ahead some fifteen years when nearly all of this group will be of reproductive age. The principle of exponential growth will be fully operative even if the average number of children per mother (6.5 in Mexico) is reduced by one-half.

As that growth develops, the population problem becomes, in turn, a "health services crisis," an "educational crisis," an "employment crisis," and so on. The problems of providing an adequate number of child health clinics or schools or jobs are challenging even to nations with more resources than most economically

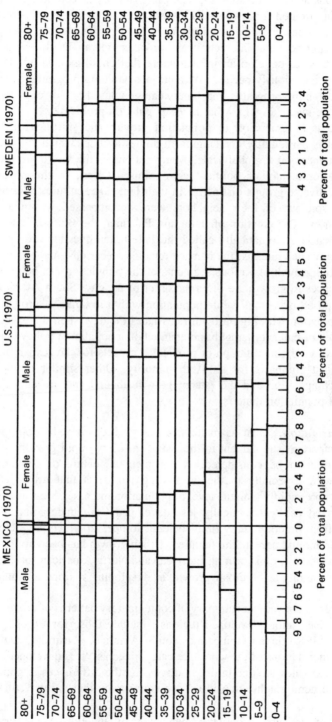

1.7A

MEXICO (1970)

1.7B

U.S. (1970)

1.7C

SWEDEN (1970)

Figure 1.7

AGE/SEX PYRAMIDS FOR SELECTED NATIONS, 1970

Source: Scientific American, 1974: 10–11.

developing nations have. Consider the choices faced by a central government between allocating limited funds to social investment and to capital investment. In the first instance, money could be provided for training persons to take their places in an industrializing economy as technicians or other operatives. In the second, funds could be used to develop an infrastructure that could expand employment prospects. Both are obviously needed. Without jobs, training programs can go for naught. Without training programs, machinery can go unused or worse. But what if choices have to be made? Again, what is *the* population problem?

Finally, there is a dimension to population growth and shifting patterns of composition that is particularly challenging to domestic order which, in turn, has political consequences on a global scale. Many nations of the world are products less of cultural logic than of political compromise. Often, in the process of nation building, diverse groups distinctive in their language, culture, religion, and politics, and suspicious of their neighbors were encompassed within arbitrary political boundaries. The creation of India and Pakistan, the Biafran civil war in Nigeria, and what is diplomatically called the Palestinian question are but a few examples. In many such nations, the balance remains precarious, and among other things, differential growth of various segments of the population can be upsetting. But such differences in growth are often the order of the day. South Africa with a population composed of a small white population with a low rate of growth and a larger black population with high growth rates faces the day when the proportions are even more out of balance. Israel has embarked on a population policy that must deal with the awkward contradiction of pronatalist aspects for the Jewish majority and an antinatalist emphasis for its Arab minority. Other similar problems of differences in composition and the rate of growth abound and are an important aspect of global population matters.

Population Distribution. Just as matters of composition must be appropriately viewed as an important supplement to the issues raised by rapid growth, so must population distribution be considered. A conspicuous feature of contemporary population growth, especially in the developing world, is that urbanization is occurring even more rapidly than the level of population increase. Most nations that can be categorized as "economically less developed" are undergoing a major transformation from predominantly rural societies to ones in which large cities are especially important and demanding features. Urban growth has been an important consideration in the past, transforming European and North American societies, but the tempo and magnitude of urban growth in developing nations are unique in human history.

Table 1.2 offers a convenient summary of contemporary patterns of urbanization. The figures for the "more developed regions" include those for Europe, North America, the USSR, Japan, temperate South America, Australia, and New Zealand. The other nations of the world are categorized as "less developed." This dichotomy approximates the one in use in discussing the differences in population growth and "the demographic transition"—a comparison that is interesting in its own right.

The key columns in Table 1.2 are the "percentage urban" for the two categories.

Table 1.2

Urban/Rural Populations, 1950–2000

YEAR	More developed regions POPULATION (MILLIONS)			Less developed regions POPULATION (MILLIONS)		
	URBAN	RURAL	PERCENTAGE URBAN	URBAN	RURAL	PERCENTAGE URBAN
1950	439	418	51	265	1,363	16
1960	582	394	60	403	1,603	20
1970	717	374	66	635	1,910	25
1980	864	347	71	990	2,267	30
1990	1,021	316	76	1,496	2,623	36
2000	1,174	280	81	2,155	2,906	43

*The definitions for "urban" and "rural" are those in use in each country. Cf. United Nations, 1969: Chapter 1. (United Nations, 1971:24).
Source: Marden, 1973: 82.

While the urban growth of the "more-developed" regions is impressive, the increases in the "less-developed" areas are especially dramatic. It is estimated that the proportion of the population of the nations that are categorized in this way will increase from 16 to 43 percent in only fifty years. Perhaps equally important, only one of every three urban dwellers will live in the cities of the more-developed regions by the year 2000—an almost complete reversal of the pattern only five decades (and almost an average person's lifetime) earlier!

These data conceal even more impressive changes in the amount and degree of urbanization, especially in developing nations. There are significant differences by individual countries in the volume and pace of urban growth. In addition, such figures conceal the enormous growth of individual cities and the tremendous challenge to the urban infrastructure (social and physical) that this represents. One wonders how India, for example, will cope with such cities as Bombay and Calcutta where the populations already exceed the size of Chicago (circa 6 million) and threaten to grow to 20 million or more by the end of the century. Similar examples abound, and behind such dry statistics rests an impressive challenge to human ingenuity in coping with this growth.

Although the conspicuousness of the pace and magnitude of urban growth is dramatic, it is paralleled by a much less noticeable, almost insidious increase of population in rural areas. In the period between 1960 and 1970, for example, the urban populations of the less-developed regions increased by 232 million—an amount that exacerbated the collective and highly visible social and physical problems faced by city dwellers throughout those regions. At the same time, however, the rural population in these areas increased by 307 million! Kingsley Davis points to the situation in Venezuela as a good illustration of the consequences here:

Its capital, Caracas, jumped from a population of 359,000 in 1941 to 1,507,000 in 1963; other Venezuelan towns and cities equaled or exceeded this (rate of) growth. Is this rapid rise denuding the countryside of people? No, the Venezuelan farm population increased in the decade 1951–1961 by 11 percent. The only thing that declined was the amount of cultivated land. As a result, the agricultural density became worse. In 1950 there were 64 males engaged in agriculture per square mile of cultivated land; in 1961 there were 78. (Compare this with 4.8 males occupied per square mile of cultivated land in Canada, 6.8 in the United States, and 15.6 in Argentina.) With each male occupied in agriculture, there are, of course, dependents. Approximately 255 persons in Venezuela are trying to live from each square mile of cultivated land.[8]

The now-developed nations also underwent a process of urbanization during their transformation to modern states but the process was comparatively gentle when that occurring in the developing world is considered. When the nations of Europe and North America underwent a revolution in agricultural techniques and organization, permitting fewer workers to produce increasing amounts of food, there was a ready market for the services of the reservoir of labor that became available. The urban centers were beginning to industrialize and the release of manpower from agriculture did not overwhelm the urban areas in their process of modernization. These cities became the centers of a transformation from a social order that was near-feudal, static, and predominantly agricultural to a society centered on "modern" values. Despite its heavy social and personal costs, the transition was comparatively smooth.[9]

The comparison is with the economically less-developed nations where urbanization is occurring without benefit of the same mitigating circumstances. Where the growth of cities in the now-developed nations was made possible by large-scale migration from the rural areas, it also solved the problems of surplus manpower in those areas and allowed for the consolidation of land into more efficient holdings. Such is not the case in the developing world. A large reservoir of labor is building up in rural areas, but at *this* point in world history, there is no demand for its services. The absorptive capacity of urban centers in Asia, Africa, and Latin America is not equal to the task and the labor situation is characterized by unemployment and underemployment. The high fertility of these nations, and the disproportionate number of young persons in their populations, provide a major economic, social, and political challenge. We might well ask again: What, then, is the population problem?

In summary, these observations about declining growth, migration, and the composition and distribution of populations have specific implications for policy and its formulation. It is important to understand that any developing (or developed) nation does not confront a single population aggregate in its decision making, but a complex matrix of interrelated problems. Each cell in the matrix may require attention that differs from that required by others and the policy-making process must be recognized as the attempt to balance such attentions. Investment in the agricultural (and rural) sector, for example, must be balanced against decisions that favor the industrial (and urban) sector. Since these decisions must be made against the background of limited resources, policy development and implementation are indeed delicate matters. A national population policy that focuses exclusively upon population size (or the related growth rate) may actually provide a disservice. A similar indictment could be made of foreign aid programs—other nation's policies—that seriously address only the problems of fertility.

Please Do Exercise 1.3: AGE-SEX PYRAMIDS

THE *POPULATION* PROBLEM

Hopefully, the preceding discussion makes a reasonable argument that there is not a single population problem despite the great attention that is directed to one dimension of the demographic changes that are taking place. In the process, the dimensions of the challenge that face us have been identified. There can be little question that population is a major global issue.

But, as our third emphasis suggests, are what we are considering really *population* matters? For some reason, many issues with a demographic component are identified in this way. That component shapes the overall perception. As noted at the beginning, Brown, McGrath, and Stokes identify 22 dimensions to the population problem ("the stresses and strains associated with continued population growth in a world already inhabited by four billion people").[10] They range from literacy, inflation, and hunger to political conflict and challenges to individual freedoms. But all of these are very complicated, multidimensional problems, and population (indeed, population growth) is but one dimension of each and, often, it is of less importance than other factors. This is not a trivial concern. But it is also not an attempt to plea bargain in hopes of reducing the charges against population dynamics. Rather, we need to avoid one-dimensional ecology in which population variables are introduced as simplistic explanations for highly complex problems. It is too easy to resort to the explanation that population growth causes or accelerates or heightens a problem. Too little effort is expended on determining the *exact* contributions of population change: and this leads to a "false consciousness" about demographic concerns. As a result, the true character of the problem (and the solutions) are obscured.

An example that illustrates this difficulty concerns changing recreation patterns in the United States. A few years ago when concern for population growth was at its height, television producers and magazine editors reached for ways to provide visual accompaniments to news stories on population issues. One convenient image of "too darn many people" was the crowding that was occurring at the various national parks. The images of long lines of automobiles, trailers, and mobile homes waiting to enter Yellowstone or other major attractions were very evocative. Clearly, if our national parks were overcrowded, there was a population problem. ("Demands for recreation" and "crowding" on the list of 22 dimensions to the population problem are appropriate here.)

Although one can hardly doubt the inconvenience of having to wait in line to see

Old Faithful and one cannot deny that the population of the United States has increased, the connection between the two requires examination. A stronger case can be made for other factors as the cause of the demands for outdoor recreation. Long before we argue about changing life-styles, we need to consider the changes in recreation in the United States over the last three or four decades. Once leisure was a luxury enjoyed only by the rich. When the system of national parks was established in the United States, the predominant pattern of summer leisure was travel by the well-to-do and their retainers to places like Bar Harbor, Banff, and Newport. Entire households moved to new locations for the summer. In contrast, other Americans either stayed home or went to Coney Island or Ocean Park for a Sunday.

In recent years, there has been a democratization of recreation. The patterns of work have changed so that vacations and opportunities for leisure are open to more than just the upper class. The increased affluence after World War II allowed persons to extend their range beyond a nearby public beach. The availability of cheap gasoline provided fuel for the automobiles, leisure vans, and mobile homes taking the trip. Many millions of Americans set off for many destinations, including the national parks. What caused the pressure on recreation: population growth or the new ability of persons to take advantage of opportunities that were heretofore reserved for a small group of Americans? Although the exact proportion cannot be easily assessed, a strictly demographic interpretation is unacceptable.

Evidence on this point can be found by examining the present patterns of recreation. Demand has shifted to the point at which the National Park Service is promoting those of its locations that can be reached through public transportation and various states are advertising the vacations that can be enjoyed on a single tank of gasoline. What has happened? There has not been a decline in population growth. One could argue that the demographic component of demand should have increased as the "baby boom" generation reached adulthood. Rather, there have been shifts in the economy and the price of gasoline that have made expenditures on leisure more problematic. The link between population growth and pressure on parks and forests is tenuous indeed!

A similar example can be drawn from the literature on population density derived from the work of researchers like John Calhoun, who considered crowding. Calhoun and others have experimented with the response of wild Norwegian rats and other laboratory animals to various levels of density. Although their research efforts deserve fuller elaboration than offered here, the basic result has been that pathological forms of behavior develop when certain densities are reached. Female rats fail to nest or take care of their young, reproductive and other behavior patterns are altered, and high levels of aggression occur. These results have received considerable attention and, with varying degrees of sensitivity to the problem of extrapolating from the experience of rats to human populations, some have used them to speculate on the consequences of rapid population growth and urbanization on humans. The specter of teeming masses of people living in close proximity with one another is a distressing image.

The problem, of course, is that it is very difficult to use the experience of wild

Norwegian rats to predict human responses to high levels of population density. Rats lack cultures, technologies, and the complexity of social structures that permit humans to respond to various social and environmental challenges. Obviously, there is some level of population density at which the quality of life—in itself, a subjective and judgmental term—would be severely challenged, but the presence of settings like Hong Kong, the Netherlands, and the upper East Side of New York City, where very high densities are maintained with relative civility and order, suggests that basing judgment about population density on a simple ratio between population size and the space available is risky. It is one-dimensional ecology.

Here we come full circle back to the question of "carrying capacity" and "optimum population" and suggest the shortcomings of such concepts. Implicit in the determination of either concept is the notion of limits to growth. Generally, these are measured in terms of environmental factors: food supply, water, minerals, and other resources. Populations grow to the point where there is pressure on these resources, and limits, capacities, or optima are reached or exceeded. Missing in the calculations, however, are various reflections of the attributes that set human populations apart from other animals: their ability to plan, organize, decide, and change. Through new forms of technology and social and political organization, it is possible to readjust the balance between population and the environment. The limits set for growth may be inevitable, but the timing at which they are reached may be a function of adaptive social organizations and technologies.

As an illustration, we need to look only to why Malthus was incorrect in 1798 in positing that population growth would outstrip the resources available to it. Malthus had little confidence in social progress ("The structure of society, in its great features, will probably always remain unchanged."[11]), and he failed to anticipate the changes in technology and organization that allowed resources to grow more rapidly in the nineteenth and early twentieth centuries than his simple arithmetic progression hypothesized: a revolution in the agricultural methods (fertilizers, plant and animal breeding, mechanization) that allowed the land to be used more intensively and productively; an improvement in living standards through industrialization, better transportation, and technological innovation; and new forms of political organization, supported by better transportation and communications, that allowed nations to be served by colonies. Malthus also failed to predict the possibility of widespread use of contraception that would cause fertility to decline.[12]

Obviously, the developments in the nineteenth and early twentieth centuries that upset Malthus' predictions were difficult, perhaps impossible to anticipate. But they illustrate the problems of striking a balance between population and resources without taking into account forms of organization and technology. That is, they suggest the dangers inherent in practicing one-dimensional ecology.

A second example that is illustrative of this point concerns the "tragedy of the commons" which is often used to reflect the problems of contemporary population growth.[13] The case concerns the common grazing lands in England which were once under great pressure because it was in the interest of individual farmers to use the land as intensively as possible. These individual interests challenged the common good and threatened the resources available through too much grazing.

Many persons who use the case to illustrate their concern about population growth focus on this challenge. Its Malthusian character and implications fit these concerns nicely. But a full examination of the case (and a careful reading of Hardin's original essay) suggests that the situation was resolved before the lands were destroyed through overgrazing. Political controls regulated the intensity with which the land was used. It was necessary for individual herdsmen to balance their interests with those of others. Some freedoms were surrendered in the interest of the common good. Although the abrogation of such rights may not fit the political philosophy of many, it does again suggest that population growth and the pressures that it places on resources cannot be considered alone. Matters of organization and technology are important elements in a complicated equation.

These examples suggest that the dire predictions about runaway population growth need to be tempered by the possibility that the balance between population and resources may be influenced by other factors. This does not necessarily lead to optimism about the demographic futures of various nations and the world because opportunities are not always seized or they may require drastic decisions that involve the sacrificing of freedoms and major alterations in life-styles. The population problem is real, but there are more than two variables involved. It is possible, for example, to reconceptualize the entire question and "solve" the population problem by requiring persons to restrict their childbearing to two and modify their consumption of all scarce resources through rationing. Then we would have problems of "freedom" or "order."

The point of raising these issues here is to stress that an appreciation of population as a global issue requires the recognition that the basic problem is more than demographic. It is not a question of raising false hopes about the future because ameliorative actions require both the vision to define the situation clearly and the ability to seize opportunities—attributes that are often politically difficult. Rather, it has three components that will shape the discussion that follows.

First, the future is not a matter of certainty. In the statistician's language, it is a case for multivariate analysis. It involves a balance between population and environment as conditioned by technology and organization. It is not enough to practice unidimensional ecology. Second, it is necessary to be tolerant of different perceptions of the problem. The willingness of many in the economically more-developed nations to impose their definitions upon others requires levels of understanding of others' histories, cultures, resources, technologies, social struc-tures, and ambitions that are usually lacking. Population problems in these nations may be as much matters of national psychology and politics as those of demog-raphy. Views of the roles that they play in the international arena should be less judgmental than has been the case. This leads directly to the third point. The policies that are proposed to deal with population issues need to be carefully assessed. If they focus on demographic variables alone, then they ignore some basic realities of political and social life.

SUMMARY AND CONCLUSION

The approach utilized in this chapter is intended to move us well beyond the point at which we began—with the conventional and simple ideas about the problems of population growth. The information about population dynamics which is convenient and comfortable is not wrong; it is just not sufficient. Ironically, one of the major difficulties about population issues is that they are easy to understand. If you add a tenth person to a room in which nine are already a bit crowded, then there are too many people! When the problem of overcrowding is expanded to a global scale it becomes a bit more abstract, but the logic seems easily transferred.

But even the facts of the crowded room may not produce consensus. Crowding is a matter of perception. For some, the arrival of a tenth person might have been quite acceptable; others would have been uncomfortable with six, or seven, or eight in the room. Similarly, crowding, for North Americans, is a negative concept. In other cultures, the definition may vary considerably. To complicate matters even more, one's place in the midst of a hundred persons behind a subway turnstile might be quite different from that among one hundred persons entering a long-awaited athletic event. What is a crowd? What is too many? What is overpopulation?

Here, we have used the term "the population problem" as a device to suggest how complicated the analysis of demographic issues might be. First, we discussed "the population *problem.*" In a sense, this presents the basic dimensions of an important global issue. The world does face dramatic and dangerous demographic challenges. The rapid growth of the world's population, the prospect for continued growth in the future, and the disparities in such growth between various nations, especially when dichotomized as "economically developed" and "developing" (or Third World), are matters that cannot be ignored by any government or thinking citizen. They help to shape the global future.

But placing emphasis on the other words in the phrase serves as a reminder that even the implications of high growth are not enough to limit our attention. "*The* population problem" is a reminder that, for many persons, there is a single demographic issue: large, indeed too large, populations produced by high growth rates. But not all nations are confronted with population increases; many have economic, social, and political problems associated with low growth or, for some, no growth at all. Further, there are many other demographic considerations that must be understood.

Finally, emphasis on "the *population* problem" was intended to raise a larger contextual issue. Population growth or population decline or shifts in age composition or any of the other demographic changes are not problems until they bump up against something. Perhaps they raise issues about the limits placed by natural resources. Perhaps they challenge the economy's ability to provide new jobs or perhaps, in the case of low-growth nations, the need cannot be met at all. But such situations are not produced by population dynamics alone. As a subjective matter, growth does not become an issue until the ability of some other variable to accommodate that growth, such as natural resources or the employment situation, is limited. We must avoid one-dimensional ecology.

So, we need to move well beyond the conventional wisdom about population matters. The symbol of the importance of doing so is the World Population Conference held in Bucharest, Rumania in 1974. In the chapters that follow, the authors return to this meeting on several occasions to illustrate a point or to aid in drawing a conclusion. The Conference challenged the commonly held views about population by demonstrating that various nations and individuals were far from consensus about the position that population growth held in economic progress and societal development. It became clear that demographic facts do not always lead to the same conclusions. A conference that some hoped would be a staging area for a worldwide campaign for fertility reduction became a platform for those with differing opinions, helping only to define the issues freshly, not to resolve them.

To organize the discussion that follows, we shall employ the four perspectives that, when taken together, can allow us to examine population as a global issue. First, we shall identify the *actors* or those who play a part both in identifying population as a problem (or as a nonproblem) and in working to reduce its impact or counteract its effects. Second, we shall identify the *values* associated with population growth. Again, values are involved in the definition of population as an issue to be discussed and acted upon since such concerns emerge when prevailing values are changed. They are also involved in defining the task of those who would seek to change patterns of demographic behavior since these are deeply embedded in individual and societal belief systems.

The third perspective is that of *policy and policymaking*. Many of the actors, influenced by particular values, work to influence others through policy. In the international area, the principal actor is the nation-state which, in turn, can attempt to influence the reproductive behavior or other demographic decisions of individuals or couples who are themselves important actors in the population drama. In turn, the nation-state, as the actor at center stage, is the target for directions from a variety of agencies ranging from international organizations like the United Nations and the World Bank to large nations like the United States or Sweden to a few individuals backed by powerful economic interests who have strongly held views about population issues. The policies that are developed reflect both the strengths of such advocacy (or resistance to it) and the values that underlie basic demographic decisions.

Finally, there is the *future*. This is the focus of attention for all of those concerned about increases in human populations. Even those who address the present consequences of rapid growth nearly always place these issues into the larger context of what will happen in the future. The potentialities of populations to grow at exponential rates condition any discussion of demographic matters. The concern is not misplaced, although the prospects for slower rates of growth in many developing nations are better than they have been in recent years. A full understanding of population futures is a requirement for all who seek to understand population as a global issue.

EXERCISE 1.1

Population Knowledge

1. At present, the population of the world is approximately

   _____.

2. It is increasing by what percentage each year?

   _____½ of 1 percent

   _____about 2 percent

   _____3.5 percent.

3. At this rate, it will double in size in how many years?

   _____.

4. These figures involve a large number of people. The problem is that it is just a number. To give you an idea of how many persons are included in one billion, figure out how many Parmas would be included. A Parma represents 100,000 persons (named after Parma, Ohio with a population of 100,216 in 1970). How many Parmas would be included in the rectangle below?

1 dot (o) = 1 Parma
         (100,000)   one billion

5. The economically more-developed and less-developed nations are growing at different rates. In the two rectangles presented below, indicate what proportion of the world's population you believe these two groups of nations have today and what it will be in the year 2000.

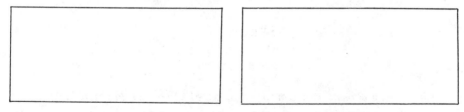

1980   2000

6. In understanding the differences between the two sets of nations, let's take one country as representative of each—the United States as an economically more-developed nation and India as one that is economically less-developed. Try to estimate the fertility and mortality of each nation.

rate per 1,000	India	United States
Births	_____	_____
Deaths	_____	_____

34

Population in the Global Arena

EXERCISE 1.2

A Demographic Riddle

Take several minutes and solve the simple "riddle" provided below. Please provide your calculations and then answer the question that the riddle raises.

Suppose you own a pond on which a water lily is growing. The lily plant doubles in size every day. If the lily was allowed to grow unchecked, it would completely cover the pond in 30 days, choking off the other forms of life in the water. For a long time the lily plant seems small and you have other things to do. So, you decide not to worry about cutting it back until it covers one-half of the pond. On what day will that be?[14]

1. Your first quick guess: The _____ day.
2. A more considered estimate. (Include your calculations.)

3. What are the implications of this little riddle for demographic understanding? What principle is involved?

EXERCISE 1.3

Age-Sex Pyramids

You have been chosen as a consultant to the Ministry of Education in Mexico. Your assignment is to estimate the long-term needs for education in that nation. They are especially interested in your ability to relate demographic information to the task at hand.

Using the age-sex pyramid for Mexico (1970), try to list the kinds of problems that nation might face in (1) maintaining and (2) expanding its present educational system. From the information provided in the age-sex pyramid, what specific pressure do you think that Mexico will face?

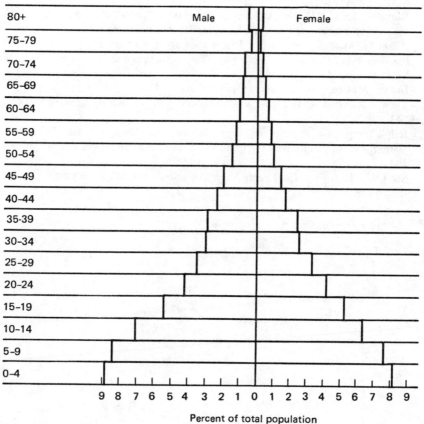

Figure 1.8

NOTES

1. Kingsley Davis, *Human Society* (New York: Macmillan, 1949), p. 545.
2. Lester R. Brown, Patricia L. McGrath, and Bruce Stokes, "The Population Problem in 22 Dimensions," in *The Futurist* X (1976), pp. 238–245.
3. Paul Ehrlich, "The Population Crisis: Where We Stand," in *Population, Environment and People,* edited by Noel Hinvilho (New York: McGraw-Hill, 1971), p. 16.
4. C. P. Snow, *The Two Cultures and The Scientific Revolution* (Cambridge University Press, 1949), pp. 48–49.
5. Davis, *op. cit.,* p. 545.

6. Kenneth C. W. Kammeger, *An Introduction to Population* (San Francisco: Chandler Publishing Company, 1971), pp. 128–132.
7. John Berger and Jean Mohr, *A Seventh Man: Migrant Workers in Europe* (New York: Viking Press, 1975).
8. Kingsley Davis, "The Urbanization of the Human Population," in *Cities,* edited by the *Scientific American* (New York: Alfred Knopf, 1965), pp. 20–21.
9. Parker G. Marden, "Population Distribution and the Green Revolution," in *Food, Population and Employment,* edited by Thomas Bleman and Donald Freebairn (New York: Praeger, 1973), p. 84.
10. Brown, McGrath, and Stokes, *op. cit,* pp. 238–245.
11. Thomas R. Malthus, *An Essay on the Principle of Population.* London, 6ed., 1826, p. 543.
12. Ralph Thomlinson, *Population Dynamics* (New York: Random House, 1976), p. 39.
13. Garrett Hardin, "Tragedy of the Commons," in *Science* 162 (December 13, 1968), p. 124.
14. See Lester R. Brown, *The Twenty-Ninth Day* (New York: W. W. Norton & Company, Inc., 1978).

chapter 2

POPULATION ACTORS

With rapid growth identified as the most pressing of global population problems, the scene shifts immediately to villages in rural India or urban slums in Caracas or bedrooms in Scarsdale where couples are making decisions about their reproductive behavior. Unlike other global issues which can be shaped directly by the actions of national and international power brokers, resolution of the problems posed by the magnitude and pace of contemporary population growth in the world ultimately depends upon the actions and behavior of a very large number of individual actors. Rapid population growth is the direct result of regular decisions made in private by literally many millions of persons throughout the world.

Hence, we are all actors in the population drama. Each of us has the potential to aggravate the problem of rapid growth just as each of us can change the distribution of populations simply by moving. Population trends therefore represent nothing more than the combined decisions of many individuals, couples, and families. And, because these decisions are shaped and conditioned by commonly held values, goals, and aspirations, there are patterns to them and the actors appear to follow the broad outlines of a script.

It is then evident that efforts to decrease the rate of population growth must eventually influence the decisions and behavior of many millions of couples if they are to be successful. Values and attitudes—the script that guides this behavior—must be altered. To be even more specific, it means that couples, overwhelmingly poor and predominantly rural, in Africa, Asia, and Latin America where population growth is so high, must choose to limit the number of their children to fewer than three and must have the means to accomplish their goal. Similarly, couples in Europe, North America, and other low-fertility regions must continue to maintain their present patterns of having small families. Each couple must stick to its decision for some twenty to thirty years, or throughout their reproductive life span. In the economically less-developed world, this decision will be one that stands in stark contrast to those made by their parents and to the weight of cultural tradition.

37

Please Do Exercise 2.1: PERSONAL DEMOGRAPHIC HISTORY

Although it is easy to forget as we consider the broad sweep of global issues, there must be no doubt that the most important actors in the world population situation are the masses. If they do not choose to have smaller families than their parents and grandparents did, then population increases will be with us until they do or until war, the lack of food, or other such factors check growth.

Despite the individual, intimate nature of the reproductive decision, the last two decades have witnessed the emergence of the network of organizations and other institutional actors dedicated to influencing Third World fertility decisions. Operating with an eye to the logical impossibility of reaching enough individual couples directly and with the assumption that national population policies are somehow important determinants of reproductive behavior, an *antinatalist* network has developed. (Here, "antinatalist" reflects any effort aimed at limiting population growth.) This network or lobby has concentrated its efforts on convincing Third World governments to adopt a variety of measures that they hope will lead to lower fertility among the citizens in the target nations. National family planning programs have been the most important feature in these concerns.

This antinatalist campaign has provoked a *pronatalist* reaction. (Here, "pronatalist" reflects those various activities, organizations, and individual actions opposed to limiting population growth.) The World Population Conference held in Bucharest in 1974 featured a confrontation among actors representing different perspectives on the population issue, not only between opponents and proponents of reduced growth, but also within the pronatalist and antinatalist camps themselves. Despite the initial hostility, however, national population policies have undergone a dramatic transformation. Twenty years ago, only a handful of the economically less-developed (or Third World) governments made even passing mention of population control or the need to limit family size. Today, nearly half of these countries (in which reside 89 percent of the Third World population) have some type of antinatalist measures on the books, and many of these governments are serious in their efforts to slow growth. The extent to which the current decline in fertility rates in the developing world can be attributed to these changes in national population policies will be examined later. In this chapter, we shall set the stage by identifying the array of actors who have been instrumental in provoking this remarkable shift in policy.

Please Do Exercise 2.2: POTENTIAL ACTORS

Our analysis considers population actors from two perspectives. First, it divides them into three groups by their activity: (1) those who attempt to *shape* global action and influence population policies in the Third World; (2) those who are the *targets* of their actions; and (3) the *observers* of these efforts. The shapers can be subdivided into those who are *antinatalist* and those who are *pronatalist* since some seek to control population growth and others are opposed both to this course of action and to the goal that it seeks to attain.

Second, the analysis examines the various actors in terms of their structure and scope. There is a bewildering array of organizations (and even some powerful individuals) operating in the international arena today. Once, the only major units involved in making global decisions were nation-states (as supported or influenced by national economic interests). Today, they are joined by organizations of nations, multinational corporations, international bureaucratic agencies, institutions and individuals within nations, and other actors all of whom have influence in the decisions that are made. To organize the discussion, we can consider three groupings of actors: (1) *international* institutions and organizations, (2) *nation-states* themselves, and (3) *subnational* institutions and individuals. Further, there are other more abstract aggregates that need to be taken into consideration: the Western developed world, the socialist nations, the Third World, and the many millions of individuals and couples whose reproductive behavior needs to be considered, or by the goals of some, to be influenced.

Table 2.1 summarizes this classification and gives examples of the more important actors. Each category is defined in the following discussion. The collection poses a confusing array of organizations and aggregates with various linkages to the others, but careful examination of these actors can tell us a great deal about the ways in which an issue emerges out of a limited constituency, gets placed on the agenda for global action, and becomes adopted as an element of national policy. It also provides insight into the limits to the awareness of global issues and policy formation as instruments for shaping individual behavior.

SHAPERS OF GLOBAL ACTION

Because they sit atop the world's organizational structure, we begin our review of those actors seeking to influence the global agenda, national policies, and Third World fertility with international organizations. While organizations in this category have played significant roles, however, the principal thrust has come from certain national actors, more specifically, the government of the United States and private North American organizations. This arrangement is, of course, quite in keeping with the configuration of power and influence in which relatively few players dominate the global scene. These national actors have effectively created and captured international organizations to represent their interests. In the case of population, after overcoming initial reluctance, the government of the United States combined forces with various nongovernmental organizations and a few influential individuals to force fertility control onto the world's agenda and then to place it in the policy inventory of most economically less-developed countries. These leaders of the antinatalist lobby have been very effective in utilizing higher level, supposedly neutral, global organizations to overcome substantial early opposition to population control.

Table 2.1
Types of Global Population Actors' Roles in Policymaking

Structure/Function	Shapers		Targets	Observers
	ANTINATALIST	*PRONATALIST*		
(1) INTERNATIONAL				
—International Governmental Organizations	U.N. Fund for Population Activities U.N. General Assembly World Bank		The Third World	The Socialist Bloc
—International Nongovernmental Organizations	International Planned Parenthood Federation World Council of Churches Multinational Dairy Companies Population Council	Catholic Church	Multinational Corporations	Multinational Corporations
(2) NATIONAL				
—Governmental	U.S. Agency for International Development	Argentina	Third World Government	Soviet Union
—Nongovernmental	Population Crisis Committee		Third World Family Planning Associations	
(3) SUBNATIONAL				
—Institutions —Individuals	U.S. Universities John D. Rockefeller III		Third World Universities Third World Couples	

International Actors

International actors represent either institutions or organizations that function at a level that transcends the nation-state. Although the character of these international bodies varies greatly, we can distinguish two basic types—governmental and nongovernmental.

International governmental organizations (IGOs), in turn, take one of two forms. They are either constituted by formal governmental (nation-state) agreement and membership with national delegations participating in a clearly prescribed manner, or they are authorized by this kind of IGO to function in a semiautonomous fashion not unlike the executive bureaucracies of national governments.

The United Nations sits at the pinnacle of the world's organizational network. If population is a serious global issue, it stands to reason that it would have been felt in the United Nations, in its General Assembly and Security Council, and within its specialized agencies. As a global issue, population should also bear the mark of the United Nations. Indeed, population growth is well established as a serious global concern in the United Nations, although much more so among the specialized agencies than at the higher levels. So, while the United Nations was somewhat reluctantly drawn into the population debate in the late 1960s, today it is a significant advocate for lower population growth. It, like other world forums, has been effectively captured by the persistent United States-led antinatalist lobby.

Until the mid-1960s the United Nations' consideration of population was restricted to technical demographic analyses carried out by a minor division of the Secretariat. In 1962, following a General Assembly debate on "Population Growth and Economic Development," a resolution was passed instructing the secretary-general to work with the member governments on their population problems. Sweden and Denmark, pioneer antinatalist advocates, were aided in their effort to mobilize United Nations action by a newly discovered and well-endowed ally, the government of the United States. Additional resolutions helped spread the population issue to the agendas of specialized agencies, such as the World Health Organization, UNESCO, and UNICEF, where important liaisons exist with member governments and subnational actors.

In order to stimulate even greater activity by the United Nations and its member governments, the antinatalist forces sponsored the creation of a new agency, the United Nation's Fund for Population Activities. UNFPA, financed by voluntary contributions, acts in a variety of ways, both within and outside of the United Nations, to keep population control on the global agenda and support policy initiatives at the international and national levels. Table 2.2 summarizes the extent and range of UNFPA support for population-related activities during the crucial early stages of the antinatalist campaign. In a larger sense, it served as a beachhead for the antinatalist forces within the United Nations. UNFPA functions, then, as a bureaucratic agency, drawing from its permanent status and full-time staff of international civil servants to concentrate on an antinatalist orientation. Like any bureaucracy it operates with a defined sense of mission and with a relative sense of autonomy. The United States government has consistently been the largest single contributor to UNFPA.

The World Bank is a second international governmental organization of impor-

Table 2.2

Contributions of the U.N. Fund for Population Activities to Global Population Programs, 1969–1972

Contributions by Type of Program	U.S. $
Basic Population Data	5,437,567
Population Dynamics	6,517,017
Population Policy	1,066,542
Family Planning	18,676,747
Communication and Education	5,891,833
Multidisciplinary Activities	3,282, 959
Program Development	5,430,540
Grants to Nongovernmental Organizations	3,806,339
Total	50,109,544

Contributions by Geographic Location	U.S. $
Africa	7,268,356
Near and Middle East	2,430,357
Asia and the Far East	16,922,151
Latin America and the Caribbean	4,467,704
Europe	171,681
Interregional Projects	15,042,956
Grants to Nongovernmental Organizations	3,806,339
Total	50,109,544

Contributions by Type of Organization	U.S. $
United Nations	16,922,759
UNDP	1,215,027
UNICEF	5,240,721
UNIDO	42,500
ILO	2,120,839
FAO	948,322
UNESCO	3,412,262
WHO	13,084,727
IBRD	400,000
IPPF	1,466,123
Allocations for Other Project Activities	1,449,925
Grants to Nongovernmental Organizations	3,806,339
Total	50,109,544

Source: Nicholas J. Demerath, *Birth Control and Foreign Policy: The Alternatives to Family Planning* (New York: Harper and Row, Publishers, 1976), pp. 55–56.

tance in the campaign to control population growth. Its leadership has been as much symbolic as substantive, with Bank President Robert McNamara (now retired), a former American corporation executive and secretary of defense, initially conducting a personal, and unpopular, crusade to lower fertility in the developing world. Speaking in 1969, he declared that "the greatest single obstacle to the economic and social advancement of the majority of the peoples in the underdeveloped world is rampant population growth."[1] Even though the Bank's concrete investment in family planning and related activities is not great, its global advocacy of population control lends legitimacy to antinatalism. Furthermore, Third World nations depending on the Bank for general developmental assistance can hardly afford to ignore its stand on population.

A third international actor is the United Nations General Assembly, which must act with more national constraints than the above two organizations. It must, for example, reflect the diverse interests of the member states. On the issue of population, this has meant that the General Assembly, dominated by Third World and socialist members, has been much slower to endorse population control measures than UNFPA, a branch of the same organization. In essence, the creation of an administrative agency, UNFPA, within an international governmental organization has allowed the antinatalist forces to sidestep considerable member opposition.

In 1974, the United Nations World Population Conference was convened to provide an international forum at which various actors could interact to shape global population policy. As the first international conference of governments to discuss population and development, this meeting proved to be instrumental in the evolution of the population issue.[2] It featured a heated debate between Third World advocates of development over population control and a United States-led coalition pushing population control as requisite to development. Immediately following the Conference, observers were quick to label the meeting a victory for one side or the other. With the passage of time, however, what seemed to emerge was a compromise, perhaps unarticulated, in which even the diehard developmentalists accepted family planning and the family planners recognized the importance of development to Third World population control efforts. The years following Bucharest have been characterized by a decline in the shrillness of the debate and widespread adoption of national family planning programs. This experience suggests the extent to which international conferences often act as a watershed in the evolution of global issues.

Among international governmental organizations, various regional organizations based on national representation and financing have also played a role in defining the population issue. One of the earliest advocates of more forceful Third World action, for example, was the Organization for Economic Cooperation and Development (OECD), a group of Western developed nations.

Like governmental organizations, *international nongovernmental* groups or organizations may take many forms as well. Some are agencies with national affiliates who consequently operate at both the national and international level. Others are simply organizations composed of individuals from a variety of nations. Still others, such as multinational corporations (MNCs) have a home base in one country but with significant branches and activities in others, and of course operate for profit.

Indeed, perhaps the most important international institution on the antinatalist side is nongovernmental in character. The International Planned Parenthood Federation (IPPF) was one of the first and most persistent voices on the international scene for population control. It has operated at two levels. At the national level, it has helped establish and maintain a network of national family planning associations throughout the world. Beginning in the 1960s, IPPF concentrated on building affiliates in Asia, Africa, and Latin America; today, virtually every Third World country has a national family planning association. These associations provide family planning services on a private, nonprofit basis (often subsidized by IPPF). In addition, they lobby in their own governments for public action. At the international level, IPPF is a dependable and effective spokesman in a variety of forums for population control (through organized and voluntary family planning programs). It is a classic example of an international interest group. IPPF receives significant financial support from the United States government, and as Table 2.2 indicates, it is linked to UNFPA.

There are also international organizations opposed to the campaign for population control. One such organization is the Catholic Church. The basis of the Church's opposition is the theological conviction that artificial contraception is immoral. The Church, therefore, opposes population policies or family planning programs that employ chemical or mechanical means—the only effective techniques for birth limitation in the eyes of most experts. This is a position that has been consistently reaffirmed at the highest level by all recent popes, including John Paul II. However, the ability of the Church to impose its position on individual Catholics and secular governments has grown increasingly problematical. Surveys show, for example, that in defiance of Church doctrine Catholic couples often turn to artificial contraceptives to plan their families. Furthermore, the authority of the Church in population matters is diluted by the fact that many parish priests and even bishops and archbishops in the Third World choose to ignore papal directives. Consequently, the impact of Church opposition on policy development is not as great as might be expected, given its firm stand on the issue and the large number of Catholics in the world. To illustrate this point, we need only consider the case of Latin America, a region in which more than 90 percent of the population is Catholic. In 1979, 20 of the 33 countries in the region had national policies that permitted population control activities, and 92 percent of the regional population were potentially covered by such policies.[3] In contrast to the Catholic Church, another religious organization, the World Council of Churches, has taken a strong antinatalist stand on rapid population growth.

Another sort of nongovernmental international actor is the multinational corporation, such as General Motors, the Shell Oil Company, or Sony, who have a home base in one nation but whose activities span the countries of the globe. The role of MNCs in global population matters, however, depends upon the goods or services that they produce. Manufacturers of products for infants, for example, might well be reluctant to endorse antinatalist measures, although there is no evidence that they have campaigned against them. Most MNCs are in fact simply observers of the global population debate, though some have become targets of global action. But their role could be greater. In a presentation to executives of the Coca-Cola Company, the deputy director of the Population Council listed the following actions that MNCs *could* do in order to help control population growth in the Third World:

1. Create jobs, especially for women
2. Adopt appropriate labor-intensive technology
3. Locate plants in rural areas
4. Support nutrition education and infant health programs
5. Provide family planning services to their employees.[4]

One multinational industry, however, that has direct vested interests in slowing Third World population growth is the pharmaceutical industry. It manufactures and sells the pills, IUDs, and other birth control devices used to control fertility. But, despite the fact that multinational drug companies manufacture, market, and even test (because of less stringent controls) contraceptives in the Third World, the industry has still not played a visible role in the global population debate.

While the role of the various multinational corporations has not been overt, the part played by three *nonprofit* international organizations based in the United States has been extremely important: the Ford Foundation, the Rockefeller Foundation, and the Population Council. Both the Ford and Rockefeller foundations, pioneers in supporting demographic and biomedical research, have financed important population-related activities throughout the world. Not being public agencies, they have the flexibility to intervene at crucial points in the policy process. From local offices in key Third World countries, these two foundations have used their considerable resources to build a population infrastructure by sending nationals abroad for graduate training, providing short courses and conferences, and helping to fund local demographic and family planning organizations. Together they have spent more than $200 million on population-related activities.[5] One of the recipients of their largesse has been the Population Council, a distinguished academically-oriented "think tank" located in New York City, where it is in close proximity and constant consultation with other participants in the global antinatalist lobby. The Population Council has helped create a network of experts throughout the world who are trained in demography and/or family planning skills and who are professionally dedicated in one way or another to analysis of and action on rapid population growth. They are found in universities, government agencies, and local family planning associations. The Population Council finances their training, subsidizes their research, and brings them together periodically in workshops and conferences. Generating objective, scientific analysis of world demographic trends has been a recent and important contribution to understanding and appreciation of rapid population growth. There are other professional or academic international organizations, such as the International Union for the Scientific Study of Population, but the Population Council with the financial support of the Ford and

Rockefeller foundations as well as the U.S. Agency for International Development (AID) is the most important of these nongovernmental actors. From 1952 through 1978, it disbursed over $187 million on population work throughout the world.[6]

National Actors

After a slow start, the government of the United States through AID has been one of the most aggressive, insistent proponents of population control for the Third World. Initially, it resisted the example set by Sweden, Denmark, and other Western European states that had been pushing for action to check population growth for some time. Then in the early 1960s, a coalition of private organizations, led by the Population Crisis Committee and their allies in Congress, convinced the Executive Branch that uncontrolled fertility was a problem—both at home and abroad, but particularly abroad—that properly required government action.

Please Do Exercise 2.3: U. S. ROLE IN SLOWING POPULATION GROWTH

The following excerpt from former President Eisenhower's written testimony presented in 1965 at the Senate's "Population Crisis" hearings neatly captures the evolution of United States government involvement in the world population movement:

> Ten years ago (1955), although aware of some of these growing dangers abroad, I did not believe it to be the function of the Federal Government to interfere in the social structures of other nations by using, except through private institutions, American resources to assist them in a partial stabilization of their numbers. I expressed this view publicly but soon abandoned it. After working and studying results of some of the aid programs of the early 1950s, I became convinced that without parallel programs looking to population stabilization all that we could do, at the very best, would be to maintain rather than improve standards in those who need our help. We now know that the problem is not only one for foreign nations to study and to act accordingly, but it has also serious portents for us.[7]

As often is the case with converts, the United States government became an outspoken advocate of population control. A special ambassador for population matters was appointed in the Department of State to press United States policy in international forums and on the governments of the Third World. More important, AID began giving foreign aid for population and family planning activities. Although AID officials deny the charge, population assistance often has appeared in the eyes of many Third World leaders as the condition for other types of foreign aid from the United States. They have resented this pressure, be it explicit or implicit; and in the early years of its campaign for population control the United States found itself as the center of a controversy, being charged with everything from imperialism to genocide. Critics asked, for example, why was the United States with its 200 million inhabitants so concerned about population growth in Mexico with only 50 million people, if not to dominate this smaller neighbor?

Undaunted, American government officials did not retreat. Now some fifteen years later, it seems probable that the leadership provided by the United States, despite a certain heavy-handedness and occasional setbacks, has advanced the cause of population control. If nothing else, the hundreds of millions of dollars granted (not loaned) to international organizations and Third World governments for population-related activities led to significant expansion of such activities. The fact of the matter is that a small Third World government could establish a national family planning program at very little cost to itself using AID grant funds. Many have done so. AID's assumption that the local government would increasingly assume financial responsibility for the program as its popularity with the beneficiaries became clear remains to be proven. In any case, as Table 2.3 demonstrates, the massive expansion in foreign aid for population-related activities that occurred after 1965 significantly reflects the leading role assumed by the government of the United States. Over one-third of all such assistance has come from this one source.

When private funds originating in the United States are added to those from the government, the American commitment to population control, in comparison to that of other countries, is truly amazing. How can we explain this commitment? Is it, as those at one extreme would have us believe, an act of genuine altruism, or is it, as the other extreme would say, a maneuver to extend United States domination of the Third World? There is probably an element of truth to both views. First, real concern exists among American officials and leaders from the private sector that uncontrolled population growth represents a serious threat to the peoples of Asia, Africa, and Latin America. Second, it is also true that national interests of the United States decisively influence policy, as the following excerpt from a State Department bulletin on "International Population Policy" demonstrates:

> In sum, the potentially destabilizing effects of excessive population growth in the years ahead must be taken seriously. Disorders abroad can affect our military and strategic situation, as well as our own unemployment, inflation rate, the prices and availability of critical industrial raw materials, and markets for our exports.[8]

A third consideration shaping United States policy has been the belief that foreign aid for economic development is wasted if population continues to grow unabated. President Johnson reflected this view when he declared that $5 spent on population control is worth $100 invested in economic growth.[9] But even here cynics were quick to point out that "Yankees" knew a bargain when they saw one and aid for development would diminish.

Whatever the motives, the prominent role played by the United States was a source of concern throughout the Third World where its actions are always questioned. This suspicion, and awareness of it, led the American government to funnel its funds for population through private institutions, such as the Population Council, and relatively autonomous (and committed) international agencies like

Table 2.3

Major Donors of Global Population Assistance, 1965–1979
(in millions of U.S. dollars)

Sources	1965–74	1975	1976	1977	1978	1979	Cumulative Thru '79
SUPRANATIONAL DONORS							
UNFPA*	168.300	64.300	73.500	81.500	101.900	111.800	601.274
World Bank	66.200	40.000	11.600	29.500	72.000	102.000	321.300
IPPF*	112.300	33.700	33.500	38.300	45.737	46.622	310.159
Subtotal*	346.800	138.000	118.600	149.300	219.637	260.422	1,232.733
TRANSNATIONAL DONORS							
Ford Foundation	156.557	10.700	10.800	8.561	7.800	6.451	200.269
Rockefeller Foundation	57.769	6.198	5.500	4.500	4.090	5.600	83.357
Population Council*	120.650	12.076	11.000	11.302	12.623	12.850	180.501
Subtotal	334.976	28.974	27.300	24.363	24.513	24.901	464.127
NATIONAL DONORS							
Western Countries (excl. U.S.)	209.414	87,030	93.037	116.640	139.836	147.117	793.074
OPEC Countries	.902	.202	7.656	1.280	1.213	.112	11.375
Other Countries	7.026	3.368	4.700	2.197	1.435	2.336	21.062
Subtotal	217.342	90.600	105.393	120.117	142.484	149.565	825.571
U.S. AID	622.369	109.975	135.460	140.250	160.540	184.935	1,353.529
TOTAL NON-U.S. GOVT.*	899.118	257.574	251.293	293.780	382.634	434.888	2,522.371
Grand Total*	$1,521.487	$367.549	$383.753	$434.030	$543.174	$619.823	$3,875.900
U.S. Govt. % of Total	41%	30%	35%	32%	30%	30%	35%

*UNFPA, IPPF, and the Population Council all receive substantial funding from the other donors in the table. They then pass this support along to other recipients. Their inclusion in the table does inflate the totals and subtotals, since it leads to double counting of some of the assistance.

Sources: Adapted from "United States International Population Policy," Population and Development Review, 6, No. 3 (September 1980), pp. 513–514. *Data for the Population Council comes from* The Population Council: A Chronicle of the First Twenty-Five Years *(New York: The Population Council, 1978), p. 210 and* The Population Council Annual Report, 1979, p. 154.

UNFPA. Meanwhile, other national governments in Western Europe continue to provide population assistance, although on a much reduced scale, as Table 2.3 documents. On the pronatalist side, national governments from the Third World will occasionally speak out against population control, as Argentina did at the World Population Conference in 1974, but there is nothing even remotely rivaling the efforts of antinatalist national actors.

Mention has already been made of antinatalist interest groups within the United States that were influential in moving the government to initiate pressure and support for population control activities in the Third World. As its name implies, the Population Crisis Committee pressed its case on the Congress and the Executive Branch as one of utmost urgency. In the words of Nicholas Demerath, "the Population Crisis Committee has been the family planning establishment's chief money raiser and Washington lobby."[10] It viewed the population explosion as a threat to world development and peace. This is an argument that the government came to accept, even when it was widely rejected in the target countries of the Third World. Other nongovernmental national actors, such as the Population Reference Bureau, were also instrumental in the United States in moving the government to take the active role that it adopted.

Subnational Actors

The story of how the international campaign to slow population growth was launched and financed extends beyond the confines of the American government and even the private interest group that lobbied it for action. Powerful individuals, such as John D. Rockefeller III, used their influence and wealth to press the case for government action, here and abroad. Once the decision was made to support the cause of reducing fertility, the United States government as well as governments of the Third World which were adopting population policies required the cooperation of a variety of subnational actors to carry out their decisions. Universities have been important in both instances. They do research, train personnel, and provide technical assistance. Most of these activities are funded through government grants and contacts. Local family planning associations are also important. It was from their small private efforts that national family planning programs often evolved.

Antinatalist versus Pronatalist Forces

The antinatalist "shapers" of global action directed against rapid population growth constitute an impressive force. In less than ten years, they have coalesced and emerged as a well-organized, well-financed global movement for population control in the Third World. The heart and soul of the movement has been the government of the United States which has bankrolled a large portion of its activities. Behind the government stands a variety of national and subnational lobbying groups keeping the pressure on for action and before it are the international agencies through which United States funds are funneled to Third World countries or which spend their own resources where funds would be unacceptable.

The pronatalist forces have proved unable to match the organization, leadership, or resources of the antinatalists. Consequently, the struggle has taken the form not so much of overcoming organized pronatalist opposition as of convincing a basically apathetic Third World that population control is in its best interests.

TARGETS OF GLOBAL ACTION

The second general category of actors in the global population drama contains those who are the targets of the antinatalist campaign, and, to a lesser degree (because of limited resources and organization), the supporters of pronatalism.

While characterized as "targets," these actors tend in fact to be rather amorphous and therefore difficult to hit. In the broadest sense, the principal target is the Third World—the economically less-developed nations of Asia, Africa, and Latin America in which population growth is rapid. Even though these countries may have policies that are varied and distinct from one another with regard to population, antinatalist groups have tended to lump them together in this widely accepted construct. But the Third World, though a convenient, if sweeping, conceptualization for speeches and other forms of rhetoric, loses its apparent clarity when one examines it more closely. In the most specific way, the targets known as the Third World are in reality those couples in villages and cities scattered throughout the less-developed nations who are making decisions about their fertility. Clearly the task in reaching the thousands of rural and urban settlements and the millions of their residents is an overwhelming one for even the most ambitious governmental agency, foundation, or health educator. The only actors in this spectrum who can realistically be targeted are the national governments and private organizations in these economically less-developed nations. In the eyes of most Western observers, those organizations represent the critical force in the drive to reduce fertility levels. This assumption, about which the final judgment is still to be made, has led to an emphasis on reshaping national population policies from a pronatalist to an antinatalist bias.

International Actors: The Third World

Despite our propensity to lump countries into a single group characterized by a convenient term, the nearly 100 nations who share the problems of being "economically less-developed"—as opposed to the "developed" status of the so-called First (capitalist) and Second (socialist) Worlds—differ along an important range of cultural, linguistic, racial, historical, social, and political attributes. In fact, it is now fashionable in some quarters to address not only countries of the Third World but to speak of a Fourth and Fifth World as well in order to account for the growing diversity of regional and economic issues. Because of this heterogeneity, it is virtually impossible for the less-developed countries, which are characterized as if they were a bloc, to actually present a consistently unified position on important global matters. This diversity has not, however, deterred the global antinatalist lobby from trying to convert these countries to the cause of population control. This has been done in a variety of ways, including the introduction of the issue into international organizations. The most direct attempt at conversion so far occurred at the 1974 World Population Conference, where there was a concerted effort to put the entire world on record in favor of a Western approach to population control.

In the case of population, while it is true that most Third World countries initially resisted the call to take action to control population growth, it is also true that some of their number, such as India, Pakistan, Taiwan, and South Korea, were among the pioneers in developing national family planning programs. Despite differences, it is possible to identify a common perspective among economically less-developed countries which is constantly reiterated at the United Nations. This view, also forged at the 1974 World Population Conference, holds that, while family planning and other fertility control measures may be desirable for a variety of reasons, including economic development, they must not be seen as substitutes for the fundamental requirements of national development. From the viewpoint of the Third World, these requirements include not only education, health, and domestic investment, but more important, the transfer of resources from rich to poor countries through more equitable aid, trade, and investment practices. This consensus has allowed for the emergence of family planning as a legitimate policy option for individual governments, but always as a measure subordinated to the central task of national development. The principal emphasis of the "World Plan of Action" enacted at the World Population Conference was on "the need for more economic and social development and for a more equitable distribution of wealth."[11] This phrase reads quite differently from the calculation by President Johnson cited above about the inexpensiveness of birth control when compared to other forms of investment in economic development.

Subnational Actors: Third World Couples

It is obvious that the reproductive couples of the Third World who produce high fertility hardly constitute a homogeneous, much less an organized, force in the world population drama. Those with the highest fertility, the rural poor, are the least organized, least influential voice in national politics, but their actions ultimately determine the rate of population growth. There are wide gaps among global pressures, national policies, and individual behavior. It is clear that Third World couples do not make reproductive decisions on the basis of their larger consequences. Rather, to the extent that it is planned—and there is considerable reason to believe that most children are wanted—family size is a function of more immediate considerations. In the context of Third World poverty, large families may be an asset rather than a liability for their parents. If the decision to have additional children is a rational one from the perspective of the parents, then the fundamental challenge of population policy is not to provide the means for limiting family size, but to provide the incentive to do so. It is necessary to replace the apparent reasons for having large families with more persuasive reasons for having small families. In the interests of advancing the cause of global antinatalism and, more important, implementing national population policies, however, it is far more complicated politically, economically, and socially to attack motivations that are strongly supported by prevailing values than it is to provide the means—specifically birth control.

National Actors: Third World Governments

Policy is the virtual monopoly of national governments in today's world. Population is no exception. Until rather recently, most national population policies and governmental measures affecting population were pronatalist in nature; that is, they were designed to, or in fact did, encourage population growth. Such an emphasis was in keeping with the widely held belief that development depended on maintaining and increasing numbers for economic (and military) advantage. The nineteenth-century experience of the United States was influential in shaping this view. Suddenly, with discovery of the population explosion, Western experts began to argue that population growth constituted an impediment to national development. This meant that population policies in Third World countries had to be reversed, an action difficult under the best of circumstances, but one rendered even more so both by the absence of internal support for such changes and by the presence of external pressures. No Third World government wants to appear to be caving in to outside pressures, especially those from the United States. On the other hand, the availability of foreign aid for population programs combined with the seeming intractability of such national problems as unemployment, inadequate social services, and massive rural-to-urban migration was an incentive to adopt family planning programs. Ideologically and symbolically, Third World governments may oppose population control; pragmatically, they have come to accept the persuasiveness of organized family planning, but usually for reasons other than population control.

Certain Third World governments have been prominent and influential in the global population debate. India, as the world's second most populous nation and the first economically less-developed country to adopt a national family program, is one. The fact that India took the first step back in 1952 made it easier for others to follow, but the problems India has encountered subsequently have likewise hurt family planning elsewhere. Mexico, with solid credentials in standing up to the United States, is another key actor. For years, the Mexican government loudly rejected the call for population control in the Third World; then just prior to the World Population Conference, it abruptly shifted its position and moved aggressively into family planning.[12] This change in policy influenced other countries to adopt family planning measures. A third significant actor in the developing world is China. Its role will be considered below. It is important to emphasize that the campaign to reshape population policies in economically less-developed nations has had rather substantial impact, despite considerable initial opposition. Much of its success involves new wrappings for the package, from the control of population growth to a family planning orientation, as it moves from providers in Western nations to recipients in the developing world.

OBSERVERS

The analysis thus far has dealt with actors in the so-called First and Third Worlds. What about those of the Second or socialist world? Many would argue that the role of the socialist countries has been curious, if not contradictory. After all, these are countries with their own strong and effective population policies. Yet, led by the Soviet Union, they are often found siding with the Third World in international forums in opposition to Western-sponsored attempts to strengthen population control. The easiest explanation for this apparent paradox is power politics,. but there is an additional factor. Marxist-Leninists do not believe in population control, but they do believe in central planning and the right of women to control their own destinies. These latter beliefs allow for the existence of birth control and abortion within a Marxist society, and at the same time a firm opposition to them as a developmental measure.[13]

China is a socialist state of special significance in world population matters. It is a nation with the world's largest population and a developing economy. Accompanying China's reintegration into the world community of nations there has been the realization that the Chinese have a strong antinatalist role in the Third World. It has also created additional confusion about the socialist position on population control, which serves to reinforce the socialist bloc's status as an observer rather than an active participant.

SUMMARY AND CONCLUSION

In the early 1960s, the world began to awaken to the fact that population was growing rapidly throughout most of Asia, Africa, and Latin America. Discovery of the "population explosion" did not, however, provoke urgent countermeasures by affected Third World governments. Rather, the initiative came from the West. A small, dedicated band of antinatalists pressured the United States government to assume financial and political leadership of the campaign to slow the advance of population growth. But, because of Third World suspicion of its motives, the United States could not deal directly with many Third World governments, much less directly with their citizens. This situation led to the creation of the antinatalist network of organizations presented in Figure 2.1. The considerable resources of the United States government, other Western governments, and North American foundations were funneled through international agencies of one kind or another into the Third World. A major milestone in the campaign was again the World Population Conference of 1974. By 1981, some 16 years after its emergence, the global antinatalist lobby was well on the way to achieving its objective of Third World population policies based on family planning.

Given the lopsided alignment of forces summarized in Figure 2.1, it is not surprising that the antinatalists have apparently won the battle over population policy. Nevertheless, an important question remains unanswered. Why was the Third World so unconcerned about the population explosion in its midst? This question shifts our attention from the population actors to their values. But in moving to values, we are again reminded that the fate of any population policy ultimately and definitively rests with the most important actors of all—the peoples of Asia, Africa, and Latin America. Unless they choose to reduce their fertility, the policies of their governments and aspirations of the international community for slower growth rates shall go unfulfilled. The initial apathy, and even outright

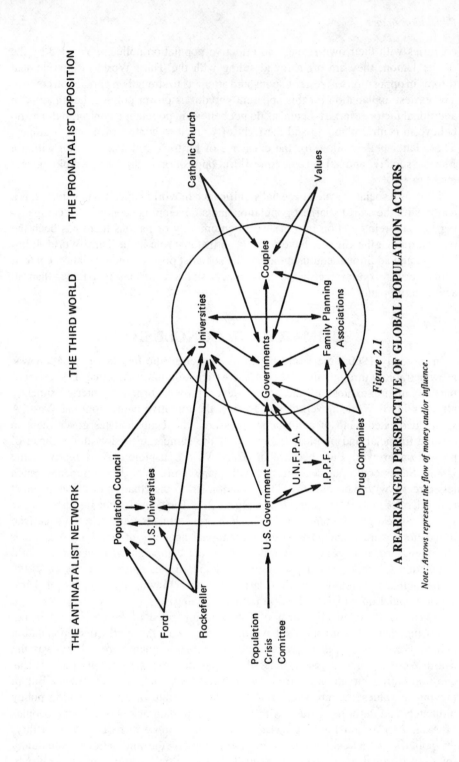

THE ANTINATALIST NETWORK   THE THIRD WORLD   THE PRONATALIST OPPOSITION

Figure 2.1

A REARRANGED PERSPECTIVE OF GLOBAL POPULATION ACTORS

Note: Arrows represent the flow of money and/or influence.

rejection, encountered by the antinatalist campaigns indicates how deeply pronatalist values permeate most Third World societies.

EXERCISE 2.1

Population Autobiography

The purpose of this exercise is to get you to reflect on the demographic experiences of you and your family and to compare them with those of the larger society. Since you may need to consult your parents for some of the information requested, this exercise will not be due for several days. It is relevant to this and succeeding chapters.

I. *Family Size History*

The following information should be provided for your natural parents. Where you are unable to provide the requested family size, place a NA in the blank and do not figure it into any averages. You should include all births, even of children who died at infancy (put them in parentheses). For example, if your maternal grandmother was one of six children, one of whom died at birth, you would enter 6 (1).

GRANDPARENTS   FAMILY SIZE

Maternal		Paternal		
Grandmother	Grandfather	Grandmother	Grandfather	
_____	_____	_____	_____	Average _____

PARENTS

| Mother | Father | |
| _____ | _____ | Average _____ |

Self and Siblings

_____   _____

Your Projected Family Size

_____   _____

Now take the data from the last column, using averages for Grandparents and Parents, and graph it with a solid line on the next page. Enter the approximate date of birth for each generation in the parentheses.

Family Size and Migration History Over Four Generations

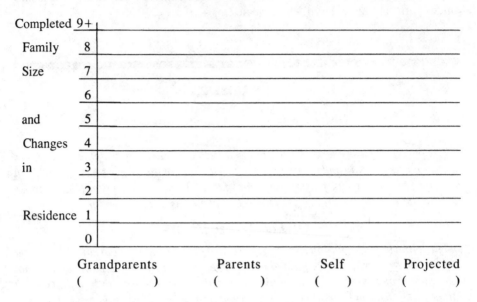

1. How does your family size history compare with that of the United States in general?
2. What are some of the reasons that might explain changing family size over the four generations analyzed?
3. Why are you going to have the number of children projected? What might affect the decision to produce a different number?
4. What conclusions can be drawn from your family size history, especially as it deviates from the norm?

II. *Migration History*

Now for each generation you are to estimate the number of changes in permanent residence beyond a 50-mile radius *made by each generation. Since you are to include all moves made from birth to death or the present, include college, since this is an important form of migration.*

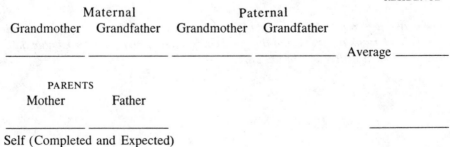

Now enter the data on the preceding page with a broken line on the above graph.

1. How does your migratory history compare with that of the U.S. in general?
2. What are the considerations that led different generations to move, if they did?
3. In what ways might family size, place of residence (as a reflection of occupation among other things), and migration interact and be reflective of common forces?
4. What do you expect for your children as far as migration is concerned?

EXERCISE 2.2

Potential Actors in the Population Drama

Without looking ahead, list five organizations (governmental and non-governmental) or individuals that might be active on the international scene in support of lower population growth, their reasons for being active, and one resource for influencing Third World population policies. Then make a similar list for five actors who might oppose efforts to limit growth and/or favor increased population growth. Your list should be based on an educated guess about the nature of the problem and the array of global actors.

ANTINATALIST ACTORS	REASONS	RESOURCES
1.		
2.		
3.		
4.		
5.		

PRONATALIST ACTORS	REASONS	RESOURCES
1.		
2.		
3.		
4.		
5.		

EXERCISE 2.3

U.S. Role in Slowing Population Growth

U.S. leadership of the effort to slow population growth in the Third World has provoked a variety of reactions. Write a one- or two-sentence response to each of the following questions.

1. What motivates U.S. leadership of the antinatalist campaign?

2. How do you, as a U.S. citizen (if you are one), feel about the use of public funds for this purpose?

3. How do you think Third World leaders and peoples feel about the U.S. emphasis on population control?

4. If the U.S. had a "population problem," how would you feel about the offer from Mexico to bring it under control?

NOTES

1. Robert S. McNamara, "Address to the University of Notre Dame," May 1, 1969, IBRD Reprint, p. 3.
2. Dorothy L. Nortman and Ellen Hofstatter, *Population and Family Planning Programs: A Compendium of Data Through 1978.* 10ed. (New York: The Population Council, 1980), p. 17.

3. W. Parker Marden, *et al.*, "A Report on Bucharest," *Studies in Family Planning*, Vol. 5, No. 12 (December 1974), p. 357.

4. Barnett F. Baron, "Population, Development, and Multinational Corporations: Prepared for Presentation to the General Assembly of Legal Counsel, The Coca-Cola Company, San Diego, December 12, 1979 (xerox copy), pp. 28–33.

5. Nicholas J. Demerath, *Birth Control and Foreign Policy: The Alternative to Family Planning* (New York: Harper & Row, Publishers, 1976), pp. 40–42.

6. *The Population Council: A Chronicle of the First Twenty-Five Years, 1952–1977* (New York: The Population Council, 1978), p. 210.

7. In David A. Baldwin, *Foreign Aid and American Foreign Policy: A Documentary Analysis* (New York: Praeger Publishers, 1966), pp. 218–219.

8. "International Population Policy," *Current Policy*, No. 171, U.S. Department of State, Bureau of Public Affairs (April 29, 1980), p. 3.

9. Cited in Phyllis Tilson Piotrow, *World Population Crisis* (New York: Praeger Publishers, 1973), p. 90.

10. Demerath, p. 42.

11. Marden, *et al.*, p. 359.

12. Terry L. McCoy, "A Paradigmatic Analysis of Mexican Population Policy" in McCoy (editor), *The Dynamics of Population Policy in Latin America* (Cambridge, Mass.. Ballinger Publishing Company, 1974), pp. 377–408.

13. J. Mayone Stycos, "Politics and Population Control in Latin America" in McCoy, pp. 7–12.

chapter 3

POPULATION VALUES

The problems of population growth and efforts to address them rest on a number of fundamental human values. Ultimately, these center upon the value placed upon children. The shift from a pattern of high to low fertility involves a major recalculation of these values. They vary from one society to another, and, accordingly, conflicts develop over perceptions of the importance to limit growth and population policies appropriate to that task. This is especially true where nations or persons with one set of values attempt to suggest or prescribe the "proper" reproductive behavior for others who are acting in accordance with other basic values.

To persons in an economically developed Western nation where small families are now the norm, it seems logical, rational, and even imperative that couples in the economically less-developed Third World should have fewer children in the best interests of their own welfare, that of their societies and of the world (including those in developed nations themselves). It is difficult to understand, much less accept, resistance to this line of thinking, but such resistance does exist. It exists not only among politicians in the Third World but also among those millions of couples that have large families. Do these people persist because of ignorance, because of an antiquated set of values, because of the blind rejection of anything with United States endorsement, or do they persist because of legitimate conditions that make large families logical, rational, and even imperative in the context of their own cultures and societies?

The purpose of this chapter is to examine the different values underlying the rapid growth of the global population, to analyze their origins and persistence, and to speculate as to how a value consensus emerged to support the widespread adoption of measures for population control in the Third World.

In considering these issues, it is important to recognize that the values with which persons approach assessments about the values and behavior of others are subjective judgments, not necessarily objective facts. Although they may be deeply held, indeed automatic in guiding one to conclusions, this does not mean that they are necessarily appropriate as the models for the behavior of others. So, it may well be profitable to review one's behavior as a "population actor" to clarify preferences and courses of possible action as well as the implied values that underlie them. Similarly, it might be useful to position this biographical review in a generational context. The choices of parents versus grandparents with respect to such matters as family size can quickly suggest how values do change. (Exercise 2.1 in Chapter 2 offered a model for your own *population autobiography*.)

The values that we hold as individuals are the product of a complex set of interactions. What is true of individuals is even more true of nations, since the latter are collections of diverse subgroups. In individuals as well as nations, values are often contradictory, in conflict with each other, and always undergoing change. Nevertheless, it is usually possible to identify the predominant values and the major countervalues of a society, to determine their origins, and to discuss their implications for an issue such as population.

Values are the products of history and tradition. We hold certain values today because they were passed on to us. Even if we modify them, the starting point is the legacy of earlier generations. Third World couples have many children because their predecessors have always done so. History and traditions are difficult to change. Values also reflect both the sacred and secular belief systems of a society. Catholics, for example, are forbidden by their religion to practice artificial contraception. They are also taught that a large family is a blessing from God. The degree to which they accept these prescriptions and proscriptions can measure their commitment to their religion. An opposing secular political ideology, Marxism-Leninism, holds that women have a right to control their own destinies by practicing birth control (although population control is not necessary in a socialist society). In turn, this is challenged by an expectation, deeply rooted in economically less-developed societies, including the industrialized nations during their early stages of development, that the first responsibility of women is to bear children.

Values are also the result of concrete conditions. The importance of children is different—regardless of history, tradition, religion, and ideology—for a couple scratching out an existence on a small piece of land in rural Indonesia than for one living in suburban Chicago. Likewise, the value of population growth is greater for a sparsely settled country like Argentina than the densely populated city-state of Singapore. Because of value differences based upon valid objective and subjective criteria, what "makes sense" for one couple or one nation may not do so for another. The large families of Americans at the turn of the century were no less rational for them than are the small families of today.

Rapid population growth originally emerged as a global issue because certain actors began to see it as a threat to their values. It persisted as a source of controversy in the international arena because other actors did *not* perceive rapid population growth as a threat to things they valued. Rather, they were more threatened by the advocates of population control than by uncontrolled population. The antinatalist lobby. led by the United States, felt that rapid population growth in the Third World was a threat ultimately to international peace since it severely hindered the prospects for national development.[1] Most economically less developed nations initially resisted the assertion that population growth was an obstacle to their economic growth and all flatly rejected the notion that their population expansion represented a threat to world peace. On the contrary, they felt that the entire antinatalist campaign constituted a threat to their national self-determination and autonomy and was a diversionary tactic to avoid the issue of international economic equity.

In the early stages of the debate, the question of basic human needs seems to have been ignored, but the policy consensus that emerged in the post-Bucharest period rested on the primacy of individual and family welfare. In essence, the actors agreed to disagree over the relationship between population and certain global values once they found a mutually acceptable value to which population policy could be anchored. What is more, population policy serves different values for different actors, a common feature of many successful policies.

The subsequent consideration of population values is based on the framework summarized in Table 3.1. It attempts to develop the relationships among general global values, population-specific values, and government population policies. In doing so it delineates four value/policy positions frequently found in the global population policy debate: pronatalist, developmentalist, family planning and population planning. Each one is described in terms of eight attributes: the basic value or character of the population, the supporting global values, the policy objective, the basic assumptions, the instruments of policy, the role of the state, the degree of political risk, and the nature of the evidence presented to support the stand. An example of a population actor supporting the position is provided. The text elaborates on each position, starting with the two more extreme stances and then moving to the two more moderate ones. Each will be illustrated with quotations from its proponents. Although the values examined in this chapter are held by various actors discussed in the previous chapter, the family planning position tends to be advanced by those in the antinatalist network while Third World actors are more likely to subscribe to the developmentalist position.

THE EXTREME POSITIONS

Pronatalist

In its most common application to a position of favoring increased population, pronatalism must now be considered an extreme stance even though it was virtually the only position for centuries. Until recently, governments considered encouraging and facilitating growth as their primary responsibility in matters of population. They attempted to accomplish this goal through such methods as direct subsidies for large families and tax penalties on bachelors, but principally they did so by encouraging immigration. Every American is familiar with the steps taken during the nineteenth century to attract foreign immigrants to "populate" the western frontier areas of North America. Similar strategies were pursued elsewhere, especially in Latin America where the slogan "gobernar es poblar" is illustrative of the belief that governing a country was equated with populating it.

Table 3.1
Alternative Value Positions on Rapid Population Growth

	Pronatalist	Developmentalist	Family Planning	Population Planning
POPULATION VALUE	Large population	Development determined population	Planned population	Controlled population
GLOBAL VALUES	National self-determination	National development and international economic equity	Basic human needs	International peace and ecological balance
POPULATION POLICY OBJECTIVE	More people	None	Rational, voluntary fertility decisions	Zero population growth
BASIC ASSUMPTION	Family size must be encouraged	Family size a function of development	Must supply means for limiting fertility	Family size must be dictated
POLICY INSTRUMENTS	Incentives/disincentives	Economic growth and income equity	Family planning clinics and population education	Incentives/disincentives, regulation
ROLE OF STATE	Promotional	Indirect	Supplementary	Coercive
POLITICAL RISK	Moderate	Low	Low	High
EVIDENCE	Developed countries	Demographic transition	KAP studies	Deductive
PROPONENTS	Argentina	Third World	USAID	China

Although never as important as immigration policies, various other measures designed to encourage high fertility have been adopted from time to time by various governments throughout the world. Even in the United States where the tide has shifted decisively against pronatalism there are still policy measures on the books that reflect the earlier mentality. The Internal Revenue Code, which awards a substantial tax deduction for each dependent, is one well-known example. These kinds of pronatalist carryovers are present in the policy inventory of most nations, not necessarily because of a continued commitment to large families but because they serve a variety of other well-entrenched interests. This persistence underlies the difficulty in fully changing public policy.

Pronatalism as a population policy value made good sense during the prolonged period of low population growth rates. However, as the world experienced the rapid growth rates of recent decades it came under attack, and the population policies of many nations began shifting in the direction of antinatalism. In the context of this dramatic reversal of traditional policy, shaped by the basic facts of rapidly growing populations, the interesting task is to explain why some actors and nations still hold to pronatalist values and policies. With them, it is more than just the momentum of the past. Rather, they are proponents of increased population growth for the present and the future.

The principal advocates of the pronatalist position tend to be the governments of large, sparsely populated countries. The South American country of Argentina is a case where the last several governments has consistently spoken out in international meetings against population control efforts. Argentina is a large country, both in terms of area and population, but one of low density and vast unsettled spaces. It also has low fertility and growth rates.[2] Thus, Argentina's demographic situation would seem to justify pronatalist values, yet such values reflect more than just the internal demographic situation. They also spring from Argentina's aspirations for regional and international power. Her leaders and intellectual elite believe that to be a great nation, to achieve real national self-determination, it is necessary both to have a large population and to fill the nation with people. Argentinians also resent a large nation like the United States promoting the belief that Third World nations should not strive for large populations. One Latin American economist of Marxist persuasion has labeled birth control as a "weapon of imperialism" and argued that:

> . . . the truth is that once the economic invalidity of neo-Malthusianism is demonstrated, it has to be interpreted as an exclusively political thesis which responds to the interests of the economically powerful countries. These interests wish to preserve the status quo and blame those people who are suffering for their own problems.[3]

Skepticism of American motives has not been limited to the left. It was, and to a lesser degree still is, characteristic of Third World nationalism in general. As recently as 1980 a high-ranking Brazilian military officer called on his country, which only recently adopted population control measures, to increase its population from 120 million people to over 200 million so that Brazil could rival the United States for leadership in the Western Hemisphere.[4] In numbers he saw strength. Such strategic considerations undoubtedly underlie the pronatalist stance of the Soviet Union and her Eastern European satellites. In the Third World they served to delay the adoption of family planning programs in countries like Brazil and Mexico that were particularly sensitive to the presence and power of the United States in their region.

Other values generate pronatalism. Not the least of these is a respect for human life. After all, population control ultimately involves the denial, either through contraception, abortion, or even abstinence, of human life. This is the viewpoint strongly supported by the Catholic Church. Yet, as pointed out, Catholic teachings on population do not seem to have been particularly influential, either at the governmental or individual levels. Similarly, the Islamic religion puts a high premium on large families with many sons, and in Moslem societies women are expected to produce and care for large families. In theory, Marxism as a political ideology also supports pronatalism for those countries with socialist systems. It sees population control as a tactic diverting attention from the real problems of the Third World, although most socialist countries do have strong and effective family planning programs. None of these value positions explicitly promotes large national populations, but they are part of an orientation that strongly resists attempts to control growth.

The irony of adhering to either extreme position, both pronatalism considered here and population planning discussed below, is that it is not easy to produce or retard population growth. For those few governments committed to increasing their populations, there are relatively few policy instruments available. When Argentina decided to strengthen the pronatalist thrust of policy, the government adopted these measures: it required that prescriptions for oral contraceptives be signed by *three* physicians; it prohibited the circulation of birth control information; and it initiated an educational campaign on the dangers of contraceptives.[5] It also resorted to a strategy used in Eastern Europe and in some Western European countries: a special bonus in the national family allowance payment for additional children and large families.[6] Beyond these concrete measures, governments usually engage in promotional campaigns, exhorting citizens to have children for the glory of the nation. This may also include symbolic rewards such as presidential recognition for a mother with more than 10 children. Just as the political risks to a government pursuing a pronatalist policy are moderate—it is unlikely to be overthrown or defeated at the polls for such a policy—so too are the prospects of success. The most decisive step it could take would be to ban abortion where abortion was previously legal, as some Eastern European governments have done, but this is often followed by an epidemic of illegal abortions.

The significance of the strict pronatalist position is that it no longer dominates the Third World. There are countries, such as Argentina, where it is not only understandable as a value, but reasonable as a policy option. Likewise, it should be pointed out again that pronatalist policies are generally ineffective in increasing the growth rate; they have been tried in Western and Eastern Europe in the face of zero population growth. Rather the significance of the position is that it reflects a number of values, held by Third World couples, which tend to inhibit the effectiveness of antinatalist policies once they are adopted.

Population Planning

At the other extreme from pronatalism, there is the value position supporting a policy of population planning. This position is gaining more individual and national adherents over time, although it is currently represented most forcefully by such nongovernmental actors as the Population Crisis Committee. The time may come when population planning, or rigid antinatalism, is not perceived as an extremist position on the population issue. But at present, the planners' emphasis on lowering the birth rate to zero through systematic and even coercive means is too drastic and politically risky for most governments to accept outright. Instead, they are beginning to incorporate bits and pieces of the repertoire of population planning while avoiding identification with it as a policy value.

The advocates of population planning see unrestricted population growth as a threat to virtually every global value; the most visible international spokespersons for the view stress that it ultimately threatens international peace and ecological balance. For example, in the Preface to the 1960 edition of his book *Standing Room Only: The World's Exploding Population,* author Karl Sax declared that:

> During the past decade, the world population has grown at an unprecedented rate. The increasing rate of population growth has been so acute that many responsible people now acknowledge that the "population explosion" is the greatest threat to world peace and prosperity.[7]

The very title of his work reflects the disastrous ecological implications he fears from unrestrained population growth.

The evidence that is brought to bear in support of the antinatalist or population planning value position is generally deductive in nature, usually based upon projection of current demographic and related trends into the future. Hence, one of the best-known treatises from this perspective, the Club of Rome computer simulation on the "The Limits of Growth" concludes that:

> If the present growth trends in world population, industrialization, pollution, food production, and resource depletion continue unchanged, the limits to growth on this planet will be reached sometime within the next one hundred years. The most probable result will be a rather sudden and uncontrollable decline in both population and industrial capacity.[8]

As has been repeatedly pointed out, many Third World leaders suspect the motives of the United States in blaming global problems on too many Asians, Africans, and Latin Americans. Indeed, in testimony before Congress in 1980, the Department of State's coordinator for population affairs stressed the threat of Third World population growth to the national security of the United States.[9] Whether one sees a threat from population growth to the entire existence of mankind or only to the security of a nation, it leads inexorably to the recommendation of

strong measures to control growth. Such a mentality led the legal counsel of Zero
Population Growth to the following conclusion:

> I submit that we cannot permit anyone to reproduce irresponsibly, and by that I mean
> have more than his fair share of the world's resources. If we permit any one person to do
> it, we can't ask anyone else to exercise responsibility. This inevitably means that we are
> going to face a form of compulsion.[10]

No Third World leader has come close to embracing publicly the neo-Malthusian
views expressed in the preceding observation nor has any Third World government
resorted systematically to compulsion to limit fertility. The political lessons of India
are still fresh in the minds of most leaders. The first regime of Prime Minister Indira
Ghandi was turned out of office by the voters partly because of its heavy-handed
attempts to force couples to limit family size. A massive vasectomy incentive
program came under particular attack. Nevertheless, increasing numbers of Third
World governments, led by those in Asia, are turning to policy measures that go
beyond voluntary family planning. The first step is typically a simple incentive
scheme that rewards a person with a one-time payment for entering a birth control
program or for being sterilized. More complex plans provide deferred rewards for
couples who complete their reproductive years with only two or three children. A
few Asian countries, led by Singapore, have even experimented with disincentives
which punish parents who have too many children by withholding social services,
such as subsidized housing and education.[11] It is the People's Republic of China,
however, which has the most comprehensive, apparently effective program for
carrying out its goal of zero population growth. The Chinese leadership justified its
commitment to "the planned control of population" as "dictated and demanded by
the socialist mode of production."[12] The means used to encourage a one-child family
include everything from rewards for those who meet the norm to penalties for those
who do not, including extreme peer pressure, required military service, and delayed
marriage.

The impressive array of policy instruments employed by the Chinese and their
apparent success in bringing down the birthrate have led many to propose China as
a model for other less-developed countries. Such reasoning fails to take into
consideration the unique configuration of demographic and political circumstances
that permit China to pursue systematic antinatalism. Other Third World governments adopting the Chinese approach would most likely experience the results of
India. We can, however, expect more piecemeal emulation of the Chinese model in
the future.

THE MODERATE ALTERNATIVES

The pronatalist and population planning positions are extreme in the sense of
being openly held by relatively few actors. They are also extreme in terms of the
policy remedies they propose and their divergence from the more accepted value
positions to which we now turn. They are not completely isolated, however,
because elements of each shade into the more moderate, middle-range alternatives.

Developmentalist

In its pure form, the developmentalist position is simply not concerned with population. Instead of being preoccupied with slowing population growth in the Third World, the developmentalists argue that the developed nations should direct their attention and resources to helping the less economically developed countries of the world to modernize and develop. They also put particular stress on the creation of a new international order in which all nations of the world share equitably in global resources. According to their argument, if these goals were to be achieved, there would be no need to worry about too many people in one set of countries and too few in another.

The significance of the developmentalist position, which was firmly held by the Third World actors at the 1974 Bucharest World Population Conference, is that most developing countries feel that Western nations, especially the United States, pay far too much attention to population growth and far too little attention to the fundamental problems of Asia, Africa, and Latin America. Furthermore, their principal concern is to maintain their position of dominance.

> Those "Malthusians" who are urging "artificial" population policies such as family planning upon poor countries do so out of a desire to direct attention from true issues of development and to thereby maintain the status quo of inequality in the world.[13]

To a degree, developmentalism is a political tactic designed to keep national development and international economic equity on the global agenda. When pushed to offer their stand on population growth, the proponents of this view recognize the existence of undesirably high growth rates, but argue that these are determined by the stage of development. Therefore, the solution to rapid population growth is the nations' economic advancement.

> Fertility will eventually decline, but as a "natural" process resulting from true social and economic development rather than through "artificial" interventions such as population policies and programs.[14]

Please do Exercise 3.1: THE DECISION TO HAVE CHILDREN

The basic premise of the developmentalists is that couples have large families not because they cannot prevent them, but because they want them. In the socio-economic and cultural context of a less-developed country, a large family is an asset rather than a liability. Therefore, the decision to have one is conscious and rational. Why might this be so? It is argued that children provide poor families in poor countries with additional income, security in old age, social status, and personal gratification. Furthermore, because of traditionally high infant mortality rates, it has in the past taken many births to assure the survival of sufficient children to fulfill these needs. Although the decision to have an additional child may carry with it adverse consequences for the nation and even the world at large, it serves the best interests of the family. Multiplying the effects of individual decisions by the millions of couples who make them, we arrive at the rapid population growth rates of Asia, Africa, and Latin America.

From this perspective, the challenge of lowering the growth rate is not to *supply* couples with the means to limit their fertility but to create the *demand* for smaller families; and the key to demand is to create a modern developed society where couples freely and rationally choose to limit family size, both because they do not need children to survive and because the family is less important in sociocultural terms.

The evidence supporting the developmentalist position is considerable. There are the differential birthrates that consistently separate the less-developed countries from the developed, and the poorer, less-developed groups within any given country from their wealthier counterparts. For example, for the period 1970−1975 the average annual birthrate for the less-developed countries was 37.5 per 1,000 but only 17.2 for the developed countries.[15] Likewise, the fertility of urban upper-middle-class couples in the Third World is very "developed" with the two to three child family being the norm. Even more compelling evidence is provided through the widely accepted historical fact that fertility rates in the West fell as these societies modernized during the late nineteenth and early twentieth centuries. Furthermore, this demographic transition occurred without modern contraceptives and organized family planning. The inescapable conclusion would seem to be that people effectively limited their fertility, even in the absence of artificial means, in response to industrialization and urbanization which stimulated the demand for smaller families.

Even though the developmentalists are quick to point out that national development is always the goal, they have modified their stand in the post-Bucharest period to allow for developmental policies that, at least secondarily, have demographic objectives. The World Population Plan of Action itself, which reflects the dominance of the developmentalist view at the Bucharest Conference, treats population as a variable to be manipulated in the development process. To be sure, the plan places importance upon development and international economic order, but it also recognizes that high fertility may need special attention.

> Where trends of population growth, distribution and structure are out of balance with social, economic and environmental factors, they can, at certain stages of development, create additional difficulties for the achievement of sustained development. Policies whose aim is to affect population trends must not be considered substitutes for socio-economic development policies but as being integrated with those policies. . . .[16]

The policy measures of the developmentalist approach that are explicitly demographic in intent are few, but they include family planning programs for those segments of the population who wish to exercise the right of voluntary fertility control. Otherwise, there is an emphasis on maximizing those aspects of national development and modernization, such as education and job opportunities for women, extended social services, and more equitable income distribution, that are conducive to lower fertility.[17] And, of course, a new international economic order is always linked to lower fertility through the mechanism of accelerated national development. Because these policies are desirable for a variety of nondemographic reasons, they are not really population policies and entail little internal political risk. Failure to deal directly with rapid population may, however, open governments to external pressures.

Family Planning

The growing popularity of the family planning position with the policymaker is partly derived from its location in the middle ground between the developmentalist approach of taking no explicit measures to control fertility and the severely restrictive proposals of the population planners. Family planning is also attractive because it serves a variety of nondemographic interests, it is voluntary, and it is often inexpensive, paid for by foreign aid. This last attraction reflects the strong financial support given to family planning by leading antinatalist actors like the United States.

Two fundamental Western liberal values underlie family planning. The first is freedom of choice. It is the family planners' contention that all couples (and especially the women because they bear a disproportionate share of the burden) have the right to choose the number and spacing of their children. Exercise of this right fulfills a basic human need. Despite identification of this principle with the West, it was incorporated in the World Plan of Action.

> All couples and individuals have the basic right to decide freely and responsibly the number and spacing of their children and to have the information, education and means to do so; the responsibility of couples and individuals in the exercise of this right takes into account the needs of their living and future children and their responsibilities towards the community.[18]

An organized family planning program, either under private auspices or directed by the state, provides the "information, education, and means" to exercise this basic right. The second underlying value is a direct corollary of this position—family planning decisions must be *voluntarily* taken. Those who espouse the family planning approach to population control therefore reject the planners' use of coercion.

These advocates also part company with the developmentalists on one fundamental point. They do not believe that development can take place without *prior* reduction of high fertility rates. They argue that the demographic transition of the West is a false analogy for today's developed countries, first, because declines in mortality in the Third World are due to external forces—for example, transfers from Western nations, rather than modernization—and, second, because Third World population growth rates are more than twice those of Europe during a comparable period. Consequently, the nations of Asia, Africa, and Latin America are caught in a "low-level equilibrium trap" in which rapid population growth slows economic development which in turn delays the completion of demographic transition to low fertility.[19] Escape from this "trap" can only occur through organized social intervention to lower fertility rates. According to the family planners, this can be done without resorting to compulsion because (and here again they differ from developmentalists) Third World couples now *want* to limit their families. They only lack the means to do so. It is a problem of supply, not of demand. To support this assertion, they point to the results of a series of KAP (Knowledge, Attitude, and Practice) surveys conducted throughout the Third World which show the parents (usually women) who want to have fewer children usually end up having more because they lack either the knowledge and/or means for controlling their fertility. If these millions of woman could be educated and provided with safe, effective contraceptives, then the population problem would be resolved.

Please do Exercise 3.2: VALUES CLARIFICATION

SUMMARY AND CONCLUSION

Because of divergent value positions, particularly between the economically developed Western world and the now-developing Third World, it is not surprising that there are differences surrounding the issue of population growth. Under Western pressure which was applied increasingly during the 1960s, the major global actors were forced to define their stands on the issue. These stands have been grouped into four population value positions as presented here. The pronatalist and population planning are polar opposites, held by those who take the extreme views in the Third and Western worlds respectively. In the middle, there are two other perspectives, the developmentalist and family planning positions, which began to converge in the mid-1970s. From this convergence has emerged a strong, although not unanimous, global consensus in which family planning is the principal instrument of population control.

The family planning position has won political acceptance throughout the Third World. There are few governments that do not have at least the beginning of a national family planning program based on a system of clinics that dispense information and materials on birth control. Besides the obvious fact emphasized in the previous chapter that there is a considerable amount of foreign aid available to underwrite family planning, the latter responds to several diverse value positions. The United States may support family planning as the remedy for rapid population growth, while the government of one of the developing countries may consider it as a social service with health consequences. Once offered, family planning is difficult to withdraw, whatever the initial motivation. The Bucharest Conference of 1974 made it acceptable, even fashionable, to combine national family planning programs with a nation's overall development effort. In recent years, some nations have gone beyond both family planning and development to adopt other measures that further integrate population and development policies.

In the next chapter, we turn to a discussion of population *policy*, that is, attempts by actors—usually national governments—to effect some change in the behavior of individuals and couples.

EXERCISE 3.1

The Decision to Have Children

This exercise calls upon you to utilize your ability to empathize. In Exercise 2.1 of the previous chapter you traced the demographic history of your family and projected decisions regarding your own offspring. Now we want you to make the family planning decisions for three different Third World couples, taking into consideration the objective conditions in which they live as well as the values that also shape their decisions.

I. *The Tapia Family*

The Tapias, Jorge, his wife, Maria, and their three daughters and one son, live on two hectares (5 acres) of rocky hillside land in the tropical country of San Marcos. Jorge's widowed mother and one unmarried sister also live in their two-room thatched shack. The land, to which they do not have legal title, is planted in corn, beans, and other subsistence crops, but even in a good year it does not support the Tapia family. Rather their margin of survival comes from seasonal employment on the neighboring hacienda of Don Ramon Garcia. Jorge and Maria have considered abandoning the countryside for the capital city, but unlike his four brothers who have already migrated, Jorge is not able to read or write. His children are able to attend the local school for three years of grammar school when they are not working in the fields. Although there is no parish priest in residence, the family considers itself Catholic. There is a government family planning center in the village, but it lacks the personnel to make home visits. Furthermore, women attending the center have complained of illness after taking the prescribed pills.

1. Jorge is 28; Maria is 23. If you were in their positions, would you have more children? Why or why not?

2. What changes in your living conditions and environment might affect your decision to have children? In what way?

II. *The Lee Family*

The Lee family is composed of Kwan Lee, his wife, Faye, her mother, and their three children, ages 6, 10, and 13. They recently moved to the provincial city of Chin, where through Kwan's brother-in-law they both were able to obtain employment in a Japanese textile factory. While they are at work, Mrs. Lee's mother cares for the children when they return from school. Although the Lees combined monthly income is $160, their rent for the two bedroom flat is $75, and food, which is constantly rising, takes most of the remainder. Furthermore, they must make monthly payments on a recently purchased TV set. Under these financial pressures, they are thinking about asking their 8-year-old to drop out of school in order to shine shoes full time. Mrs. Lee does have access to a birth control clinic, as part of the government's social security program.

1. Kwan is 30; Faye 28. In their positions would you have any more children? Why or why not?

2. What changes in your personal situation and/or the larger society might influence your decision?

III. *The Hossain Family*

The Hossains, Amir and his wife, Shushum, live in a tiny Cairo apartment. They have been married for three years and have no children, a fact that considerably disturbs each set of parents. Both Amir and Shushum are college graduates; in fact, they were the first in their families to attend college. He is a civil engineer working for one of the many American companies active in Egypt in the last several years, while she is a sociologist employed by the Ministry of Education. Both have been offered fellowships to pursue graduate studies in the United States. With her husband's consent, Shushum has been taking birth control pills prescribed by her private physician.

1. Both of the Hossains are 27 years of age. In their positions, would you have children, when, and how many?

2. What are the factors in their life-style that tend to produce very different family planning decisions from those of either the Tapias or Lees? How could the Tapias and Lees achieve the same status as the Hossains?

EXERCISE 3.2

Value Positions

Consider each of the following statements. After each of them you are to list those value positions (pronatalist, developmentalist, family planning, and population planning) that are consistent with the statement.

VALUE POSITION

(1) All women with three or more children will be sterilized. _____

(2) All families with more than two children will pay a 5% income tax per child. _____

(3) Birth control methods will be taught in the schools. _____

(4) Abortions will be made available at governmental expense. _____

(5) Government information that ascertains whether the parents can afford any additional children will be made available to parents. _____

VALUE POSITION

(6) The government will provide day care centers free of charge so both parents can work.

_____

(7) Free lifelong medical care will be made available to all citizens.

_____

(8) The government will jail for six months any parents or children born out of wedlock.

_____

(9) Parents who wish to have children must obtain a permit from the government before conception.

_____

Now consider the following actors (you may want to consult Chapter 2): China, Argentina, Rumania, IPPF, U.N. Fund for Population Activities, USAID, Catholic Church, President Lyndon Johnson, World Bank, Third World couple. For each of the above ten statements, list those actors who would support the position represented. Be prepared to justify your selections.

(1) _____

(2) _____

(3) _____

(4) _____

(5) _____

(6) _____

(7) _____

(8) _____

(9) _____

(10) _____

NOTES

1. See Harf and Trout, *Understanding Global Issues: A Framework for Analysis* volume in this series.
2. Terry L. McCoy, "Introduction" in McCoy, ed., *The Dynamics of Population Policy in Latin America* (Cambridge, Mass.: Ballinger Publishing Company, 1974), pp. xix–xx.
3. Jose Consuegra, "Birth Control as a Weapon of Imperialism," in McCoy, p. 164.
4. *Latin American Weekly Report,* April 16, 1980, p. 12.
5. *New York Times,* March 17, 1974.

6. In Argentina, general family allowance payments increased 30 percent with 100 percent increase for large families, births, and adoptions. The First National Bank of Boston, *The Situation in Argentina,* April 3, 1974. "The city government of Paris has recently offered to grant about $300 a month to Parisian mothers who will give up their jobs in order to bear a third child." Miami *Herald,* July 20, 1980, p. 11G.

7. Karl Sax, *Standing Room Only* (Boston: Beacon Press, 1960), p. ix.

8. Donella H. Meadows, *et al., The Limits to Growth: A Report for The Club of Rome's Project on the Predicament of Mankind* (New York: Universe Books, 1972), p. 23.

9. "International Population Policy," in *Current Policy,* No. 171, U.S. Department of State, Bureau of Public Affairs (April 29, 1980), pp. 3–4.

10. John C. Montgomery, "The Case for Compulsory Regulation of Reproduction," in *The World Population Crisis: Policy Implications and the Role of Law* (Charlottesville, Va.: The John Bassett Moore Society of International Law, 1971), p. 73.

11. United Nations Fund for Population Activities, "The Role of Incentives in Family Planning Programmes," in *Policy Development Studies,* Number 4 (1980).

12. Chen Muhua, "Birth Planning in China," in *Family Planning Perspectives,* 11, No. 6 (November/December 1979), p. 350. The author is a vice-premier of the People's Republic of China and director of the State Council Birth Planning Group.

13. W. Parker Mauldin, "Report on Bucharest," in *Studies in Family Planning,* 5 No. 12 (December 1974), p. 363.

14. *Ibid.*

15. Dorothy Nortman and Ellen Hofstatter, "Population and Family Planning Programs: A Factbook," in *Reports on Population/Family Planning,* Number Two (8 ed., October 1976), p. 5.

16. Mauldin, *op. cit.,* p. 381.

17. William Rich, "Smaller Families Through Social and Economic Degrees," in Colin I. Bradford, Jr. *et al., New Directions in Development* (New York: Praeger Publishers, 1974), pp. 193–287.

18. Mauldin, *op. cit.,* p. 383.

19. Henry M. Roulet, "Family Planning and Population Control in Development Countries," in *Demography,* VII (May 1970), pp. 214–215.

chapter 4

POPULATION POLICY

Population policy refers to deliberate government attempts to influence one of three demographic *process* variables—fertility, mortality, or migration—or, through them, to shape three *structural* variables—size, composition, or distribution of population. Although this perspective directs attention to the actions of the state, it should be remembered that a number of actors affect the formulation of population policies. Nonetheless, the state remains central. In the second half of the twentieth century, it is the one actor considered capable of altering the demographic dynamics of large populations, a viewpoint that was reaffirmed at the World Population Conference in 1974. The state is then the focal point. International actors attempt to influence demographic dynamics by influencing the decisions of nation-states. Subnational actors—individuals, families, and communities—are basically perceived to be those whose behavior warrants national policy intervention, although administrative subdivisions within nations (such as states or provinces) may also have the power to enact their own population policies.

Please do Exercise 4.1: GOVERNMENT POLICIES

VARIETIES OF POLICY

Historically, the demographic variables of mortality and migration have attracted the most government attention. With respect to mortality, the state has traditionally considered the reduction of death and disease to be a major national goal. Many interventions—for example, the implementation of public health measures such as the construction of sewers and water works or disease control programs such as quarantines and innoculation programs—have been undertaken by the state almost since its inception. With the advent of international organizations, attention to death and disease was relatively noncontroversial, and organizations like the World Health Organization and the Pan-American Health Organization have been major world forces even while other international agencies were embroiled in controversy. The adoption of policies to control death have elicited great consensus among all actors about the desirability of the goal.

Efforts to affect migration patterns also have a long tradition. Attempts to influence who enters and leaves national territory can be traced back many centuries. Currently, every country regulates immigration by concerning itself with the number and kinds of persons who enter it legally. The state has also attempted to influence the movement of people within its boundaries through the implementation of various laws and programs. The English Act of Settlement of 1662 is a classic example of such an attempt. This Act sought to keep people in the area of their birth by offering welfare payments only to those who remained in their home parish. The Homestead Act of 1862 in the United States is another good example of an internal migration policy, in this case inducing people to move to frontier areas by offering free land. Although the specific content of government population policies to influence migration patterns, particularly immigration/emigration policies, has often proved controversial, a general consensus has developed among a wide variety of actors that the formulation of such policies is a legitimate function of the state.

By far, the most controversial area of government population policy, however, has emerged in state attempts to influence fertility. The earliest such attempts were pronatalist policies. Several Western nations, most notably France, have a long history of attempting to increase national birthrates by offering material incentives to induce couples to decide to have children. These policies responded to fears of depopulation and a weakened economic and military position. Such pronatalist policies are becoming increasingly common today among low birthrate countries, particularly in Eastern Europe. The controversy with regard to pronatalist policies centers around their effectiveness. There is little evidence that pronatalist policies have worked, although Rumania, which virtually prohibited abortions in the fall of 1966 after having permitted and subsidized them prior to that time, did succeed in increasing its birthrate for a time. Within a short period, however, couples turned to more private means of birth limitation and the declines in fertility resumed.

Even more controversy surrounds the most recent attempts to influence fertility by the state: fertility reduction policies. Prior to 1950, there had rarely been an explicit national policy aimed at limiting human fertility. But by 1979, governments involved in the destiny of more than 2.4 billion of the world's inhabitants had population policies aimed at lowering fertility. Currently, over three-quarters of the population residing in the economically less-developed nations, or the so-called Third World, lives in countries that have an official fertility reduction policy.

Controversy surrounds this policy for three reasons. First, there is no agreement among all actors regarding the goal of fertility reduction policies. Many individuals, families, communities, religious groups, cultural groups (and even a few states or provinces) do not feel that smaller families are something to be desired. Governments attempting to lower fertility thus face the opposition of many of their own citizens. Second, there is also controversy of a more academic nature regarding fertility reduction policy. Can such a state policy actually bring down national birth-rates? If birthrates can be reduced by state intervention, will modernization efforts be greatly facilitated? These questions have yet to be definitively answered and, therefore, this debate over fertility reduction policies continues. Third, controversy abounds because nearly all the economically developed nations of the world advocate fertility reduction policies for their counterparts in the developing world. Many Third World nations question the motives behind their support. Do developed countries truly wish the Third World to experience comprehensive modernization? Or do they simply wish the Third World to stop increasing in population size because it threatens their own interests?

Although government policies influencing mortality, migration, and fertility are all significant in terms of contemporary population dynamics, our treatment of population policy will focus upon the controversy surrounding the fertility reduction policies of Third World nations. The global "population crisis," especially as represented by the rapid growth of developing nations, surfaced during the postwar era much like a volcanic island emerging from the ocean's depths. Although tremors had been felt for some time, no one was truly prepared for the awesome and threatening development that came into view after World War II. Even as it was watched closely, the dimensions of the "crisis" continually grew in size and finally assumed monumental proportions. Rapid population growth in the Third World has now emerged as the major demographic issue of the twentieth century. As a consequence, population policy has come to be seen mainly in terms of attempts to lower this rate of growth by means of "population control." For most Third World nations, rapid population growth can be humanely lowered in only one way: fertility reduction. Migration on the scale needed is not feasible and mortality increase, as a policy option, is untenable. A discussion of population policy in the 1980s, therefore, must be mainly concerned with two issues: the "crisis" of rapid population growth in the Third World and the major policy initiatives associated with fertility reduction.

FERTILITY REDUCTION POLICIES IN THE THIRD WORLD

There are currently 132 Third World countries with populations over 100,000. Thirty-five of these have adopted official policies aimed at reducing population growth rates by lowering fertility (see Table 4.1). These thirty-five countries tend to be large, together possessing over three-quarters of the developing world's population. In Figure 4.1, it can be seen that nearly all the heavily populated countries of Asia are members of this group: China, India, Indonesia, Pakistan, Bangladesh, the Philippines. (Please note that Figure 4.1 is a map of the world in which each country's size is proportional to its annual number of births, not to the extent of its geographic area.) Thus, Figure 4.1 dramatically illustrates that Third World countries possessing large populations have generally adopted explicit fertility reduction policies.

An additional thirty-one countries from the total, containing 14 percent of the

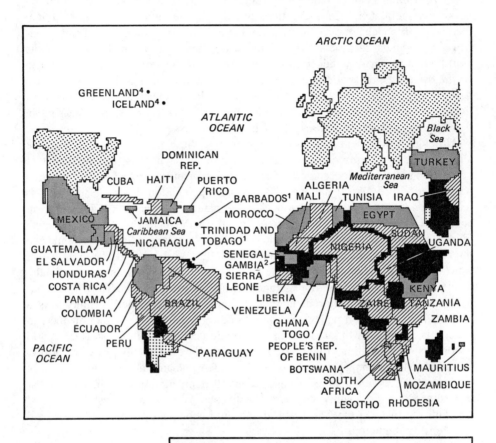

ARCTIC OCEAN

GREENLAND[4] •
ICELAND[4] •

ATLANTIC
OCEAN

Black
Sea

TURKEY

Mediterranean
Sea

DOMINICAN
REP.

CUBA   HAITI   PUERTO
RICO

BARBADOS[1]

ALGERIA   MALI   TUNISIA   IRAQ

MOROCCO   EGYPT

MEXICO

JAMAICA
Caribbean Sea   TRINIDAD AND
NICARAGUA   TOBAGO[1]

SUDAN   UGANDA

NIGERIA

GUATEMALA
EL SALVADOR
HONDURAS
COSTA RICA
PANAMA
COLOMBIA
ECUADOR
PERU

SENEGAL
GAMBIA[2]
SIERRA
LEONE
LIBERIA
VENEZUELA
GHANA
TOGO
PEOPLE'S REP.
OF BENIN
BOTSWANA

ZAIRE

KENYA

TANZANIA

ZAMBIA

BRAZIL

PARAGUAY

PACIFIC
OCEAN

MAURITIUS

SOUTH
AFRICA
LESOTHO   RHODESIA

MOZAMBIQUE

1	Official policy to reduce population growth rate.
2	Official support of family planning activities for other than demographic reasons.
3	Balance of developing world. (Names and boundaries of countries in this category are not shown.)
4	Areas generally with low fertility, whether economically developed or developing. (Names and boundaries of countries in this category are not shown.)

Figure 4.1

**GOVERNMENT POSITION ON POPULATION GROWTH AND FAMILY
PLANNING AMONG DEVELOPING COUNTRIES**

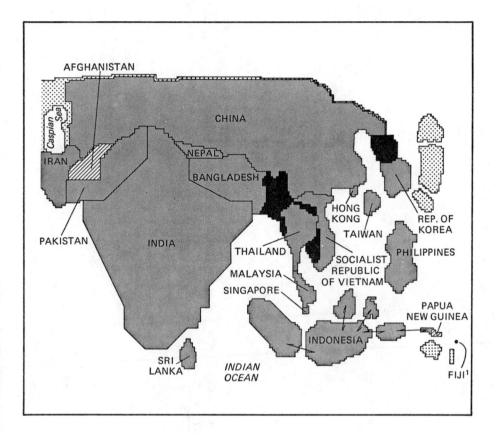

Each country's size is proportional to its annual number of births.
Source: Dorothy Nortman and Ellen Hofstatter, Population and Family Planning Programs: A Factbook, *8ed. (New York: The Population Council, 1976), Figure 1, pp. 52−53.*

Table 4.1

Government Positions on Population Growth and Family Planning in Third World Countries, 1979

Government position[a]	All developing countries[b]	North Africa[c]	Balance of Africa	West Asia[d]	East Asia and Oceania[e]	South Asia	Latin America[f]
NUMBER OF COUNTRIES[g]							
TOTAL	132	6	46	16	25	6	33
Official policy to reduce the population growth rate	35	3	5	2	11	5	9
Official support of family planning activities for other than demographic reasons	31[h]	2	15	2	1	0	11
Government position unknown	1[h]	0	0	0	1[h]	0	0
Remainder: no policy to reduce the growth rate and no support of family planning activities	65	1	26	12	12	1	13

Note: Data shown in this table are for developing countries that have official government population policy positions (see footnote a) or that have estimated populations of 100,000 or more.

a   Government positions are based on the latest available information.

b   Development status is based primarily on stage of economic development. Argentina, Uruguay, and Israel, classified as developing by the U.N., are omitted from this table because they have had low birthrates for several decades.

c   Includes Algeria, Egypt, Libya, Morocco, Tunisia, and Sudan.

d   Excludes Israel, which has low fertility.

82

PERCENTAGE DISTRIBUTION OF POPULATION							
TOTAL	100	100	100	100	100	100	100
Official policy to reduce the population growth rate	77	63	10	54	94.0	99.9	36
Official support of family planning activities for other than demographic reasons	14	35	58	19	0.2	0	56
Government position unknown	1	0	0	0	1.2	0	0
Remainder: no policy to reduce the growth rate and no support of family planning activities	8	2	32	27	4.6	0.1	8
1978 POPULATION (IN MILLIONS) TOTAL	3,109	103	339	146	1,373	828	320

Source: Nortman and Hofstatter, 1980.

e   Excludes Japan, Australia, and New Zealand, which have low fertility. Includes Melanesia, Polynesia, and Micronesia in Oceania.

f   Includes the Caribbean area plus Central and South America but excludes Argentina and Uruguay, both of which have low fertility.

g   The count of countries with neither a policy to reduce the growth rate nor support of family planning activities excludes countries with high fertility having populations under 100,000.

h   Democratic People's Republic of Korea.

Sources: Data derived from D. Nortman and E. Hofstatter, 1980 Population and Planning Programs: A Compendium of Data through 1978, 10ed. (New York: The Population Council).

Third World's population, have government-supported family planning activities but no explicit policies advocating fertility reduction (see Table 4.1). In these countries access to fertility control measures is viewed as a basic human right and/or a valuable health service. Government support is given to family planning activities for these reasons, not because a lower birthrate is desired by the state. Figure 4.1 shows that many of the large countries of sub-Saharan Africa and Latin America fall into this group: Nigeria, Zaire, Tanzania, Brazil, Venezuela, and Peru. In fact, Table 4.1 indicates that a majority of the population of these two regions resides in countries that support family planning activities but lack an explicit fertility reduction policy.

There are an additional sixty-five Third World countries that have neither a policy to reduce population growth nor a program of government support for family planning activities (see Table 4.1). These sixty-five countries, however, contain only 8 percent of the Third World's population. Figure 4.1 shows that many of the smaller nations of sub-Saharan Africa, the Middle East, and Latin America fall into this category. Most of these countries simply do not view their current rates of population growth as being detrimental to their development efforts.

Included in these sixty-five countries are several that have active pronatalist policies. They have enacted laws and implemented programs aimed at achieving high fertility levels. Saudi Arabia, for example, desires a larger labor force and in 1975 banned the import and sale of contraceptives. Laos, a country of only 3.5 million people surrounded by larger neighbors, saw many of its citizens flee to Thailand during the 1970s to escape military conflict. It, too, has banned birth control. In 1979 the Chilean government, disturbed by a declining birthrate, renounced its former support for family planning activities and assumed a pronatalist stance. In general, Third World countries with pronatalist policies are few in number, have small populations, and together contain a minuscule proportion of the Third World's population.

THE IMPLEMENTATION OF FERTILITY REDUCTION POLICIES

Although there are thirty-five countries that have explicit fertility reduction policies, the content of these policies varies greatly. China, for instance, desires to achieve zero population growth as soon a possible. In pursuit of this goal, the government penalizes couples who have more than two children and rewards couples who have only one child. Colombia, also desirous of lowering its population growth rate, has adopted a strictly voluntary means of attaining that goal: providing individuals with the means to decide freely and responsibly regarding the number of their children. Clearly, the meaning of the term "fertility reduction policy" differs from country to country and incorporates a number of distinct approaches.

Family Planning Programs

The most common means of implementing a fertility reduction policy has been to establish a family planning program. Such programs attempt to reduce fertility by making knowledge about fertility control, contraceptives (usually oral contraceptives, IUDs, and condoms), and often sterilization procedures and abortion all accessible to the public. The success of such programs has varied greatly. For instance, in Bangladesh only 9 percent of married women aged 15 to 44 use contraceptives, while in Hong Kong 79 percent of these women are users.[1] If a family planning program is to lead to a significant reduction in fertility, obviously a substantial proportion of married couples must make use of the services being offered. Countries that rely upon family planning programs as the cornerstone of their fertility reduction policy are assuming that a substantial proportion of high-fertility groups are already desirous of limiting their family size and simply lack the means to accomplish their goal.

A number of countries have decided that a more aggressive program is needed than simply providing family planning information and services if the fertility of their citizens is to be substantially reduced. Often, a family planning program is accompanied by a government-supported propaganda campaign to convince the population that small families are more desirable than large families.

Where there is state control of the media, opinions differing from that promulgated by the state are often banished from newspapers and from radio and television broadcasts. Propaganda campaigns have played a central role in the fertility reduction efforts of China, India, Indonesia, and South Korea.

"Beyond Family Planning" Programs

Programs that are more directly coercive than propaganda campaigns have also been implemented. These programs are characterized as either "population planning" or "beyond family planning" as identified in the preceding chapter. Systems of incentives to limit family size and attendant disincentives to having many children have been put into effect by a number of states. There have also been cases where national and local governments have developed negative systems of sanctions and pressures to induce couples to limit family size. Some of the more notable examples follow.

Please do Exercise 4.2: THE 1,000 PESO FINE

China.[2]   China wishes to achieve zero population growth as early as 1985 but no later than the year 2000. Its population policy slogan is "later (marriages), longer (time between births), and fewer (children)." The minimum age of marriage is 23 for women and 25 for men. Early marriage is discouraged by penalizing those who marry young, restricting their ability to attain housing, and limiting their opportunity for admission to universities.

Currently, China is attempting to induce couples to have few children by penalizing those who have more than two children and rewarding those who have only one child. Couples having a third child suffer a 10 percent pay cut until the child reaches fourteen and they are denied free medical care and education for the third child. In cities couples who promise to have only one child are granted a monthly stipend until the child is fourteen. They also receive preferential treatment in attaining an apartment, being given living space equal to that given a two-child family, and are eligible for a special pension upon retirement (equal to 80 percent of their preretirement wages). The single child is also granted an adult grain ration and special consideration in school admission and job placement. In rural areas, couples promising to have only one child are granted additional monthly workpoints (pay) until the child is fourteen. All rural couples, regardless of family size, are granted the same size private cultivation and housing plots (an allocation based upon a four-person family).

Each province is allocated an annual "birth quota." At the local level, public meetings are held to determine which couples will be permitted to have a child that year. Generally, the birth quota is allocated by granting permission first to childless couples, then to couples with one child over the age of two, then to couples with one child under the age of two, and so on. Local officials monitor every couple's contraceptive practice and great pressure is brought on those becoming pregnant out of turn to get an abortion.

Singapore. [3]   Singapore desires to reach zero population growth and has adopted a program of incentives and disincentives to bring this about. The measures to "dissuade" couples from having large families include a smaller income tax deduction for the third child and none at all for any children beyond the third. No preference is given to large families for subsidized housing and indeed few large apartments are constructed. Charges for the delivery of children beyond the first are higher and no paid maternity leave is provided for working women who already have more than one child. Measures to reward couples who have small families include granting parents who have been sterilized after the birth of their second child special rights in choosing primary schools for their children, and allowing only small families to sublet rooms in their apartments. Special monetary rewards are also granted those who undergo sterilization.

India. [4]   The Indian fertility reduction program has experienced several shifts in policy during the 1970s. The family planning program under the first administration of Indira Gandhi included both the use of incentives and disincentives. Cash payments were made to those undergoing sterilization procedures. For example, payments of 100 rupees (about $12.60) were made to males undergoing vasectomies at special vasectomy camps. In 1975–76, the central government set "sterilization targets" for each state and district commissioners were required to achieve the target by any means possible. In many instances this resulted in the use of pressure tactics and coercion. Government officials used their powers to grant employment, school admissions, permits, and licenses to recruit candidates for sterilization. There were even instances where physical force was used. Great political opposition to the Gandhi government resulted from this program and some observers trace the election defeat of her party to the implementation of this more "coercive" fertility reduction program.

The succeeding government of Moraji Desai reverted to a purely voluntary program in 1977 and there was a substantial decline in the number of participants. In 1979 the Desai government reinstated cash payments of 6 rupees ($0.76) for IUD insertions and 70 rupees ($8.82) for sterilizations. Indira Gandhi later returned to office, but it was not clear what changes, if any, would be made in the family planning program.

Indonesia.[5]   Indonesia desires to have a birthrate in 1990 which is half that of its 1970 rate. The government has attempted to mobilize communities behind its fertility reduction effort. The majority of the population reside in 3,500 hamlets (banjars). Each banjar has a "hamlet acceptor group" and a contraceptive distribution center. A birth reduction target is given to each banjar and peer pressure is used to achieve that goal. "A map of all houses in the banjar is prominently displayed in the meeting hall, identifying the method of contraception used in each household. Contraceptive practice is discussed at each monthly meeting of household heads, and nonusers are asked to justify their behavior. In some banjars, the banjar leader daily sounds a drum to remind women to take their oral contraceptives."[6]

The Philippines.[7]   The Philippines desires by the year 2000 to have each woman, on the average, bear only two children. To begin working toward this goal the government doubled its expenditures for family planning between 1974 and 1978. A number of "beyond family planning" measures have also been implemented: tax exemptions are now limited to only four dependents; maternity leave benefits are granted for only the first four deliveries; establishments with more than 300 employees must offer free family planning services; and "population education" has been included in school curricula. The central government has also attempted to involve other levels of government as well as communities in its fertility reduction efforts. One result of this effort is that currently over 200 municipalities require proof of "family planning counseling" before a couple can obtain a marriage license.

The Future of "Population Planning" Programs

The use by states of more intrusive intervention in pursuit of fertility reduction is a trend that has gained momentum recently. As can be seen by the above examples, such efforts at family planning intervention are found mainly in densely settled nations of eastern and southern Asia. These nations were among the first to identify the existence of a "population problem"; they were among the first to adopt official fertility reduction policies, and they are among those states giving the largest state support to family planning programs. India was the first state to adopt an official policy for limiting fertility (1952), followed by Pakistan (1960), the Republic of Korea (1961), and China (1962). Since the population residing in these countries constitutes over 60 percent of the entire Third World population, this meant that by 1962 the majority of the people living in the developing world were in nations having fertility reduction policies. Throughout the remainder of the 1960s and 1970s, scores of additional states—Middle Eastern, Latin American, and African as well as Asian—adopted official fertility reduction policies and began state-supported family planning programs. If this past sequence of adoption is repeated with the interventionist strategies of "population planning," then perhaps the 1980s will see such interventions moving beyond Asia and spreading to other regions of the world.

To some extent, the past sequence had its roots in the changing definition of the "population problem" which took place during the postwar era. The "problem" grew from being a peculiarly "Asiatic" problem to an endemic Third World problem. With each passing decade, a larger and larger portion of the Third World came to be seen as suffering from this problem and more and more countries adopted fertility reduction policies in an attempt to help resolve the problem. It is then the nature of the "population problem" that again allows us to understand why governments adopted fertility reduction policies, why the sequence of adoption moved from the east to the west, and why controversy continues to surround these policies.

POPULATION "PROBLEMS" AND THE DEVELOPING WORLD

Following World War II, demographic trends in the economically less-developed nations became a matter of increasing concern both to their own governments and to the governments of more developed countries as well. Mortality declined significantly, fertility remained high, and rates of population growth sharply increased. In terms of the demographic transition, these nations were in the phase of "transitional growth." Starvation, malnutrition, disease, poverty, economic stagnation, illiteracy, unemployment, and political instability were all problems that were considered by some to be flowing from these demographic trends. However, the concern about population did not arise solely out of consideration of any particular demographic characteristic—whether size, growth rate, or age distribution. As stressed in Chapter 1, population became an issue calling for action only when viewed in connection with other factors. Table 4.2 presents a series of combinations of population characteristics and "other characteristics" that have resulted in perceptions of "population problems." (The following discussion is keyed to this table by number.)

Population Size/Limited Resources Problems (Equations 1 and 2)

In the late 1940s, India's large and rapidly increasing population size was viewed in conjunction with its limited arable land, and the specter of more people than food appeared to many. A number of policymakers began to consider this combination of factors as "the population problem" of India. The limitation of population size appeared to them as the key to solving the problems of famine and malnutrition.

Because of similar occurrences of such population/resource relationships throughout Asia, the population crisis was thought during the 1940s and 1950s to be a peculiarly "Asiatic problem." Would food and natural resource supplies be adequate to feed, clothe, and shelter large and dense populations which were growing larger and more dense? Would there be sufficient resources for such

Table 4.2

Population Problem Equations

Population Characteristic		"Other" Characteristic		Problem
1. Large population size	+	Limited arable land	=	Food shortage, starvation, malnutrition
2. Large population size	+	Limited resource base (petroleum, coal, iron ore . . .)	=	Population/ Resource handicap to improving living standard through industrialization
3. Rapid population growth	+	Low level of economic development	≈	Population "stumbling block" to rapid economic development
4. Very young population (consequence of rapid population growth)	+	Limited public funds for vital public services	=	Difficulties overcoming illiteracy, improving health conditions, and increasing rates of economic growth
5. Rapid population growth disrupts land tenure system, movement from countryside to city increases	+	Low level of industrialization	=	Unemployment Underemployment Overurbanization Marginal population Political instability

populations to urbanize and industrialize even if their basic needs could be met? It is not surprising that facing such questions, the first Third World governments to adopt "population policies" to deal with these problems were in the large and densely settled countries of southern and eastern Asia, such as India, Pakistan, and China.

Rapid Population Growth/Economic Development Problems (Equation 3)

At the same time, during the 1950s, there was also a growing awareness of the rapidity of recent mortality declines in the Third World and of the historically unprecedented levels that population growth rates had reached. This awareness brought forward a new set of concerns which revolved around the detrimental consequences for economic development seen to result from the high rates of population growth themselves. No matter how small a country's population size might be, with population increasing at a 3 percent annual rate the economy would have to increase at an equal rate simply to make sure that the already low standard of living would not slip even lower. An economic growth rate of considerably more than 3 percent would be needed if there were to be significant short-run improvements in levels of living.

At this time, economists concerned with economic development placed great emphasis on the role played by "capital accumulation" in the development process. The economies of nations in the Third World were viewed as being less-developed because the average worker had little "capital stock" with which to work. Peasants farmed with hoes, not tractors. Construction workers dug foundations with shovels, not bulldozers. Economic development was seen as being a process of adding to the capital stock of the average worker. Thus it required that economic surpluses be invested in the construction of factories that would produce the necessary tractors, bulldozers, or other technological improvements. Rapid population growth made it necessary, however, to invest economic surpluses in more food, clothing, and shelter in order to feed, clothe, and house the growing population. Rapid population growth, therefore, came to be considered by most economists as an onerous burden placed upon the backs of the already capital-starved economies of the Third World.

Age Structure/Development Problems (Equation 4)

When demographers subjected rapid mortality decline to a careful scrutiny, they arrived at a finding that served to reinforce this concern for the way that population growth challenged economic development. Countries with high fertility rates, like those in the developing world, have traditionally had a high proportion of their population in the younger ages. Although common sense might lead one to suppose that a decline in mortality would increase the average age of a population, this was found not to be the case. The most marked improvements in life expectancy were occurring within the youngest age groups and infant mortality rates were declining especially rapidly. The proportion of the population in the productive ages (approximately 15 to 64) actually declined as the proportion of those under fifteen increased. By the end of the 1950s it was not uncommon for a developing country to have more than 45 percent of its population under the age of fifteen.

Many economists considered a situation in which there was nearly one person in the nonproductive ages for every individual in the economically active years to be a "demographic stumbling block" to efforts at economic development. Such ratios were considered to place limits on a country's potential for capital accumulation simply because nonproducers made up such a large proportion of the population. Also, such a young population made it necessary for a large proportion of a country's available investment capital to be used to meet "demographic investments" (investments in the goods and services, especially education and health care, needed by the young if they are to grow up to be productive citizens) rather than for more directly productive purposes.

By the end of the 1950s, then, the perception of the "population problem" had undergone a decided alteration. High population growth rates came to be perceived as having a direct negative impact on economic development efforts. Population size and density considerations were no longer used to isolate areas having a "population problem." All Third World countries experiencing rapid population growth, irrespective of their current size and density, were assumed to be demographically handicapped in their struggle to modernize. Latin America, the fastest growing region of the world during the postwar period, came to be considered by many to be an area having a particularly grave "population problem."

Rapid Population Growth/Employment Problems (Equation 5)

By 1970, many Third World countries had been experiencing very high rates of population growth for twenty years or longer. By this time, significantly larger and larger cohorts of younger people were entering the labor force each year. Some developmental experts began to see a new population problem in this phenomenon—the beginnings of a "global unemployment crisis." The issues of "overurbanization" and "marginal populations" appeared usually lumped together with the employment problem. But all of these issues are really differing aspects of the same phenomenon: the fact that stable employment in the nonagricultural sector was not being created at a fast enough rate to absorb the increase in the nonagricultural (principally urban) labor force resulting both from the natural increase in high fertility and low mortality and from the movement of people away from agricultural employment.

In the villages of the Third World, when babies were born, they survived instead of died, and when they matured, they found that land was not available for all of them to stay in their place of birth. Many were forced to make the move from the countryside to the city. But the city, while it offered the chance to eke out a livelihood, was often not equipped to offer productive jobs, adequate housing, or even basic services such as water and sewers to the many rural migrants arriving in ever increasing numbers. The "demographic" explanation of this phenomenon placed the major blame on rapid population growth. The "demographic" solution to the problem involved the need to lower the birthrate so as eventually to lower the rate of growth of the labor force.

IS "POPULATION" THE PROBLEM?

As indicated in Chapter 1 and as can be seen from Table 4.2, there is no one "population problem" facing the Third World or any particular country. There is a whole series of problems that some people argue have population variables as their root causes. There is disagreement, however, on this point. There are those who minimize the importance of the population characteristic as a real cause of each of the problems contained in Table 4.2. It is possible to find examples that "refute" the validity of each of the equations contained in that table.

For example, Equation 1 posits that there is a relationship between population density and food shortage. The Netherlands, however, has a population density 175 percent that of India, yet food shortage does not result. Instead, trading relations relieve it. Equation 2 argues that there is a relationship between large population size, limited natural resources, and the potential for industrialization. Yet Japan, with its large population and limited natural resources, has become industrialized and now possesses a high standard of living. Equations 3 and 4 contend that rapid population growth and the high dependency ratio it produces are "demographic stumbling blocks" to economic development. Yet Mexico, with its high rate of population growth and young population, has experienced a much more rapid rate of per capita economic growth over the last thirty years than Chile, with its lower rate of population growth and older population. Equation 5 contends that rapid population growth leads to high levels of unemployment. Yet countries following a socialist model of development (China, for example), even when possessing demographic characteristics similar to other Third World countries (India, for example), do not seem to have similar problems of unemployment and "marginal populations." The point is not to debate each position since that would require more detailed analysis than is possible here. The point is to stress that the matter is more complicated and uncertain than it appears on the surface. Table 4.2, however, does fairly reflect the evolution of concern for population problems.

Rapid Population Growth: A Cause or Consequence of Underdevelopment?

Even within academic circles, there is some disagreement on whether population variables should be considered as root "causes" of the problems listed in Table 4.2. For most of the twentieth century, demographers viewed the fertility, mortality, and population growth levels of a country as variables that were largely *determined* by the level of economic development of that country. That is, demographic trends were viewed as being *consequences* of economic trends. This perspective is embodied in the demographic transition model presented in Chapter 1. In its classic form, this model theorizes the following sequence of demographic change: mortality decline, followed by rapid population growth, then, after some lag, fertility decline and the gradual cessation of growth. Those who saw transition theory as a causal model posited that this sequence would occur as societies underwent a transformation from traditional agrarian conditions to modern, industrial ones. Demographic change, particularly fertility decline, was considered to be a subsidiary component of the general modernization process.

In the transition model sequence, mortality is shown to respond quickly to the altered socioeconomic conditions brought about by urbanization and industrialization. With increases in the standard of living came improved nutrition, better housing, and a decline in death rates. The pace of population growth quickened. As the processes of urbanization and industrialization continued, however, birthrates gradually declined. In the city, children were less and less likely to be the economic assets for their parents that they had been on the farm. What is more, with the passage of child labor laws and compulsory education laws, children became definite economic liabilities for their parents. As the economy diversified with the rise of industrial society, the opportunities for advancement multiplied. More and more of the population entered the competition to improve their position within society. Back in 1907 a respected sociologist observed that "to the climber, children are encumbrances, and so the ambitious dread the handicap of early marriage and a large family."[8] With the decline in fertility, the pace of population growth slackened. Demographers considered this decline in fertility to be the result of individuals consciously restricting their family size in response to changed socioeconomic conditions.

All the original formulations of transition theory contained an explanation of Third World population dynamics that also considered their demographic characteristics to be *consequences* of their economic condition. During the 1940s, the vast majority of Third World countries were still colonies of already developed countries. The socioeconomic changes that had transpired in colonies under the economic and political domination of advanced industrialized powers were considered to have profound demographic consequences: mortality decline, no fertility decline, and an increase in population growth.

Demographer Frank Notestein, generally credited as one of the originators of transition theory, noted in 1945 that colonizing nations sought colonies "as a source of specialized raw materials and as markets for manufactured goods." To achieve these ends they installed strong centralized government structures, improved the means of communication, implemented certain sanitary and epidemic control measures, and improved the productivity of agriculture. The demographic consequence of these actions was "population growth without substantial increases in the level of living." Industrialization was inhibited and there was little change in family structure, in the religious belief system, or in the aspiration levels of the populace. As Notestein summarized:

> In short, the modern nations of the West have imposed on the world's nonindustrial peoples that part of their culture which reduces mortality sufficiently to permit growth, while withholding, or failing to foster, those changes in social setting out of which the reduction of fertility eventually developed in the West. The result is large and congested populations living little above the margin of subsistence.[9]

The consternation aroused among demographers by Third World population trends during the postwar period was not due to the lack of a theoretical framework that could explain them. In fact, much of the consternation was due to the existence of such a framework. For it was especially within the context of transition theory that the demographic trends of Third World countries appeared so ominous. Most economists were arguing that rapid population growth was hindering industrialization efforts. Industrialization, according to transition theory, was the one change proven capable of inducing fertility decline and the eventual cessation of population growth. Under the influence of transition theory, demographers were therefore forced to make predictions of disaster when forecasting the future population trends of the developing world. Population growth was projected to continue until it was eventually halted by famine, disease, or war.

By the 1950s, most demographers were actively calling for population control measures to be instituted in Third World countries. From the perspective of transition theory, the social structure of Third World societies had not been altered in such a way as to bring about fertility decline "naturally." Without active intervention aimed at lowering fertility, catastrophe seemed inevitable. Population control was needed if there was to be economic development. Thus demographic trends came to be seen as *determinants* of economic trends, rapid population growth as a *cause* of underdevelopment.

Can Government Policies Bring Down Birthrates?

Could fertility decline then be induced in societies that were still primarily agrarian? Could Third World governments enact population policies that would induce peasant couples to have smaller families? Although transition theory implied that this would have to happen if catastrophe was to be averted, it also implied that it might be impossible. If decisions regarding family size were largely determined by the socioeconomic situations in which couples found themselves, were not peasant couples still living in a situation where benefits flowed to those with large families? Were not children still a source of unpaid labor, of old-age and accident insurance, of salaries that could be added to the family's income? Was not the peasant without children or with only one son still to be pitied? As demographers called for population control measures, they did so more out of a humanitarian hope that such measures *might* work than out of a conviction that they *would* work.

The question of whether the government can bring down the birthrate of a peasant population has been hotly debated during the postwar period. It was a major point of discussion at the World Conference on Population held in Bucharest in 1974. By 1974, family planning programs had been in existence in a number of countries for a substantial period of time. Why, one might ask, could these questions concerning the effectiveness of such programs not be answered by reference to actual events? The events of the preceding decades were such that no definitive answers to these questions were forthcoming. True, during that time a number of countries (Taiwan, South Korea, Singapore, Puerto Rico, Malaysia) had experienced noticeable fertility declines, had developed national family planning programs, and had undergone significant economic development. But this very confluence of events allowed both the advocates and critics of the family planning programs to draw very different conclusions from the same facts.

The advocates argued that the conclusion to be drawn from this was that family planning programs worked; birthrates had been lowered. The critics noted that those countries had all been experiencing economic transformations and that birthrates were declining not in response to the presence of family planning programs, but in response to changed socioeconomic conditions. Birthrates had not come down in the still agrarian populations, places like India where a family planning program had been in existence for some time. These critics argued that direct interventions aimed at lowering fertility were not working. They argued that the indirect method of inducing development, with the gains to be shared even by the poorest sections of society, would be a more effective means of lowering fertility. Such arguments found a sympathetic audience, given the desires and suspicions of Third World delegates.

Since 1974 it has become increasingly clear that birthrates have begun to fall in a range of Third World countries, even in countries with limited degrees of economic development. The most dramatic evidence that direct intervention by the state can bring down birthrates comes from China. Although there is no way to verify independently the accuracy of demographic statistics released by Chinese officials, descriptions of the program in place and the magnitude of the recorded decline in local fertility leave no doubt that a substantial national fertility decline has occurred. Chen Muhua, vice-premier of the People's Republic of China and director of the State Council Birth Planning Leading Group, stated in 1979 that "China's birthrate has dropped from 40 per thousand in the past to 18.43 per thousand. . . . Our rate of natural increase has fallen from 2.3 percent in 1971 to 1.2 percent in 1978."[10] A drop in fertility of such magnitude in so short a time and in a basically agrarian country is totally unprecedented. As described earlier, China's fertility reduction program does not rely solely on a voluntary family planning program, but incorporates a whole range of incentives and disincentives as well. Chen Muhua relates that a goal of .5 percent rate of natural increase by 1985 (a more than halving of the 1978 rate) has been set. To accomplish this goal an attempt will be made to stop all couples from having more than two children, and to induce many couples to have only one child.

Therefore, the question of whether government fertility reduction policies can bring down birthrates must be answered with a tentative yes. It is tentative because success seems to be dependent upon the state's possessing sufficient power to work its will over its citizens. In countries where a sizable portion of the population is engaged in nonagrarian pursuits and where economic development is proceeding, it is difficult to apportion what percentage of fertility decline is due to socioeconomic change and what percentage might be due to the government's program. In large, low-income, agrarian countries, such as those found in large parts of Asia, governments have tended to move beyond family planning programs in their attempt to lower fertility. Varying amounts of "coercion" are being applied. The Chinese example indicates that such policies can bring birthrates down. Yet, when the government of Indira Gandhi moved in this direction with its sterilization program in 1976, it was replaced by a new government which returned to a voluntary family planning program. There was a substantial fall-off in the number of participants. Although Mrs. Gandhi also returned to power, it remained to be seen whether the Indian fertility reduction program would resume a more coercive course. The continued success of China's program, then, is likely to be dependent upon the continued strength of the government. If great internal discord arises in China, the success of the fertility reduction program is likely to be threatened, as was the case during Mao's Cultural Revolution of the 1960s.

The recent fertility decline experienced by China has greatly strengthened the case made by demographers who argue that fertility reduction policies can work. From a global perspective, however, the question has yet to be definitively answered. In many areas of the world, birthrates have not yet significantly declined, even when fertility reduction programs have been in place for a number of years. In areas where birthrates have declined, it is still too early to tell the extent to which they have been permanently reduced by government programs. The potential of government programs for fertility reduction, particularly in primarily agrarian settings, is still a controversial question among those who discuss population policies.

Rapid Population Growth: How Great a "Stumbling Block" to Development?

There is also a debate over fertility reduction policies among economists, most of whom have considered high rates of population growth to be a major "stumbling block" to economic development efforts. These economists note the very high rates of economic growth needed to produce real increases in per capita income under conditions of rapid population growth. They focus on the difficulty of attaining high rates of capital accumulation in the presence of the very young population that results from high fertility levels. Yet to document the negative impact of population growth on economic growth, they cannot simply point to a strong correlation between these two rates of growth in the "real" world. When rates of population growth and rates of per capita economic growth are examined for Third World countries, no strong association between the two is found.[11] Moreover, population growth and economic growth have not historically affected one another negatively.[12] If rapid population growth were a major stumbling block to development, should not Third World countries with the highest rates of population growth also be those with the lowest rates of per capita economic growth? The weak association between the two rates has raised questions about the impact of population growth on economic development efforts.

The documentation used by economists wishing to illustrate the negative impact of population growth on economic growth tends to take the form of simulation models that artificially "project" what would happen to a country's rate of economic growth if birthrates fell.[13] The findings of such studies are very much influenced by assumptions about the nature of the development process contained within the model. Hence, simulation studies showing a profound negative impact of rapid population growth on economic growth have been criticized for making unrealistic assumptions concerning the greater capital requirements caused by rapid population growth.[14] In some cases, only a slight modification of the assumptions contained in the model can produce dramatically different conclusions about the relationship between population growth and economic growth.[15]

If there are significant declines in fertility in Third World countries during the 1980s, then what is presently an academic controversy centered on mathematical models might assume greater impact. If, in the real world, a reduction in fertility and lower rates of population growth turn out not to have a significant impact on rates of economic growth, then Third World interest in fertility reduction policies might lessen substantially. This might especially be so for the less densely settled countries of Africa and Latin America where concern over population growth does not arise from population/land or population/resource concerns. Of course, if there are great economic benefits associated with fertility declines, interest in such policies will be heightened.

THE POLITICS OF FERTILITY REDUCTION POLICIES

As is by now evident, controversy does exist regarding the true nature or the real extent of contemporary population problems. And this controversy is not limited to abstract questions but spills over and surrounds all aspects of population policy. In the arena of international relations, questions regarding who or what is truly responsible for food shortages, underdevelopment, high energy costs, global employment problems and the like necessarily take on political overtones. At international meetings, like the Bucharest Conference in 1974, these overtones have surfaced in both the writings of scholars who give different weights to the population component of contemporary problems and the speeches of politicians from developed and developing countries who differ as to what should be done to solve them.

The controversy involves both priorities and emphases. There are few today who believe that rapid population growth is not contributing at all to the difficulties facing the economically developing nations. And there are few who do not foresee the necessity of bringing to an end the current period of rapid population growth in the Third World. However, there is great disagreement over how much "blame" for these difficulties should be placed on rapid population growth and how much on a variety of other factors. There is also great disagreement over how quickly the rates of population growth have to be reduced—that is, how high on the list of global or national priorities the control of population should be placed. Should priority be given to bringing down birthrates? Or should priority be given to economic development efforts which, if successful, will induce birthrates to fall "naturally"? It is mainly around these areas of disagreement that the controversy swirls, not those areas of consensus.

Two Worlds, Two Views

If there is economic underdevelopment in the Third World, what has to be done to end it? Does economic development require a widespread population control effort or does it require a change in the economic relationship between the Third World and more developed nations (a new international economic order)? If food shortages develop in the Third World, what action should be taken by nations like the United States that have grain surpluses? Should they willingly give the food needed to prevent starvation? Should food be withheld, since preventing starvation now might simply lead to a worse catastrophe in the future? Or should food be given with certain "strings" attached—for example, the requirement to institute significant population control efforts? What about the employment problems of the Third World? Does a solution require the cessation of population growth? What if developed countries paid higher prices for the exports of the Third World? What if developed countries lowered tariff barriers on the labor-intensive commodities (such as textiles, shoes, agricultural products) that Third World countries can produce at competitive prices? Would jobs then develop for these now "redundant" workers?

If one adopts the view that the Third World problems of underdevelopment, malnutrition, and unemployment are fundamentally "population problems," then both the cause and the solution of these problems are to be found within the Third

World itself. The answer seems simple: high birthrates are causing the problems and fertility control programs can solve them. All that the developed world needs to contribute is the modest amount of money and technical advice it takes to establish fertility control programs capable of reaching the bulk of the population. Such a view of Third World problems has great attraction to policymakers within the developed world.

But if one views the problems of underdevelopment, malnutrition, unemployment, and rapid population growth in the Third World as being fundamentally caused by the ties of dependency that have bound and still bind the Third World to the developed world, then the solution to these problems requires a global redistribution of power and wealth. A new international economic order in which developed countries no longer strive to maintain exploitative relationships with less developed ones is needed. Such a solution requires much from the developed world. If significant redistribution does not take place, then global chaos, only one element of which is an "overpopulated" world, is likely to result. Such a vision of Third World problems has great attraction to policymakers in the economically less-developed nations.

When Western advocates of fertility control speak to Third World audiences, their words are often greeted with suspicion. From the Third World perspective, emphasis upon the need for fertility control is a ploy of the developed world to sidetrack efforts to address the "true" causes of Third World problems: dependency and exploitation. Even representatives from Third World countries with strong fertility control programs will often voice objection to talk of Third World "population problems." Advocacy of global fertility control has come to be identified as a developed world's policy position. Considering the origins of this policy position, there is some justification for this identification.

Origins of a Global Fertility Reduction Policy

As discussed earlier, during the late 1940s and early 1950s certain demographers and economists began calling for active intervention to reduce Third World fertility. Within these disciplines Third World population dynamics came to be seen as inherently problematic. Continued high fertility coupled with declining mortality had produced a global "population crisis," a condition of instability that would become catastrophic if it continued unchecked. The work of these academicians, however, is not what placed the population crisis high on the world's agenda of global concerns. Only when certain individuals and private foundations made substantial funds available to promote the cause of fertility reduction policy throughout the world did this begin to happen.

In 1952, John D. Rockefeller III founded the Population Council. The following is a recollection of the original mandate given to the Council staff:

> When the Population Council was founded in 1952 the trustees made it clear that their interests were world-wide and directed the staff to "take initiative in the broad fields which in the aggregate constitute the population problem." Believing as they did that

the mounting tempo of growth among the world's poorest people represented a major threat to social-economic development, to political stability, and indeed to human freedom, they were concerned with the problems of population growth in poverty areas both at home and abroad.[16]

During the 1950s and up until 1965, the monies of private foundations, particularly the Rockefeller Foundation and the Ford Foundation, funded the bulk of research, training, and demonstration projects in population control/family planning. University-based "population centers" sprung up in both developed and Third World nations nourished by these funds. The literature on the Third World's population problem increased dramatically.

After the mid-1960s, the U. S. government and various United Nations agencies, especially the U. N. Fund for Population Activities (UNFPA), replaced the private foundations as the major international financial supporters of Third World fertility reduction activities. During the 1950s, such activities were still considered quite controversial and government leaders, even in developed countries, shied away from supporting them. President Eisenhower did so out of consideration for Roman Catholic attitudes: "When I was President, I opposed the use of Federal funds to provide birth control information to countries we were aiding because I felt this would violate the deepest convictions of a large group of taxpayers."[17] By 1966, however, President Johnson argued in support of such use of federal funds on the grounds that high population growth rates "challenge our own security. They threaten the future of the world."[18] The crisis perspective on Third World population growth had thus percolated up to the highest levels of government leadership in the developed world and the scale of funding for fertility reduction activities increased dramatically. Since controversy still surrounded the issue of population control in the Third World, the 1970s increasingly saw developed nations channeling their funding through intergovernmental agencies such as the UNFPA rather than directly dispersing the aid themselves.

Within Third World nations, the usual sequence of events that eventually led to the government's adoption of a fertility reduction policy began with various foundations granting fellowship support for its nationals to study demography at university-based population centers, generally located in a developed nation. Here, they studied under Western demographers and economists and they soon absorbed the crisis orientation toward current Third World population dynamics. Funds would then be given for mounting a KAP survey (knowledge, attitudes, and practice of contraception) in that nation. In general, these surveys collected information that could be interpreted to mean that a substantial majority of all respondents were interested in learning methods of fertility control. These surveys seemed to document the existence of a "ready market" for birth control and so provided a "scientific" demonstration that establishing a family planning program might actually lead to a decline in fertility. The KAP survey also was a persuasive instrument that was potentially capable of altering the views of national elites who were doubtful of the feasibility of a fertility reduction program.

After the results of the KAP survey had been analyzed and distributed, a demonstration family planning project was usually started. A national Planned

Parenthood Association, with financial and technical assistance from the International Planned Parenthood Federation, might establish a limited number of family planning clinics within the country. Several years of operations of such "private" clinics were usually sufficient to demonstrate to the government the feasibility of establishing a national operation.

By 1970, a dozen economically more-developed nations were providing substantial funds that were explicitly earmarked for subsidizing such activities and therefore the cost of such a program for the national treasury was minimized. (See Table 2.3 in Chapter 2 for the major sources of population assistance during the 1970s.) Often, government leaders had already felt pressure to adopt a fertility reduction policy from the World Bank and other international actors. The path of least resistance led many Third World states to adopt a fertility reduction policy. Of course, some Third World states, especially China, also came to adopt such policies on their own.

Thus, the notion that world stability was threatened by rapid population growth and that a concerted effort should be made to lower fertility had its origins in the developed world. The individuals, foundations, and governments advancing this positon have played an important role in the spread of policies intended to limit births in high fertility countries. But they have not succeeded in convincing Third World leaders that a global crisis exists and that aggressive action is needed. In fact, suspicion has mounted concerning the developed world's support of fertility reduction policy. This suspicion became manifest at the 1974 Bucharest Conference.

The Future of a Global Fertility Reduction Policy

With each passing year, as additional Third World states adopted fertility reduction policies, many observers thought that the Bucharest World Population Conference would be the place where consensus and wide support might be developed in favor of a global policy to reduce rapid rates of population growth. This did not take place. But rather than unity and agreement Bucharest produced controversy and division. The "worlds" divided. The Third World viewed with suspicion the First World's concern about controlling its population growth. The call by the Western, economically more-developed world for a united effort to lower fertility was met not with agreement, but by the Third World's cry of "development is the best contraceptive," a call for a united effort to forge a new international order in which development would be for all and the population problem would wither away.

The Third World's slogan was not meant as an argument against fertility reduction programs and there was no dismantling of programs after the Conference. In fact, since 1974, a number of additional Third World countries have adopted explicit fertility reduction policies (Guatemala, Senegal, and Vietnam) while still others have come to give government support for family planning activities (Mozambique, Peru, Sierra Leone, Togo). In over a dozen countries, the government's own expenditures for fertility reduction programs have more than doubled since the Conference, with several governments more than quadrupling expenditures.[19] Instead, the slogan was meant to highlight the major concern of all

Third World countries: development is the primary objective. Fertility reduction is not an inherent good or a primary objective. A national fertility reduction policy only makes sense when it is an integrated component of a national development policy. A "global" fertility reduction policy makes sense only in the context of a "global" commitment to universal development. Without such a commitment, it is a policy to be viewed with suspicion.

The message to the developed world was clear: concern about population growth must be coupled with an even greater emphasis on development, otherwise the "concern" is suspect. The decade preceding Bucharest had seen a dramatic increase in the developed world's funding of fertility reduction activities. It had also seen much slower growth in the developed world's level of funding of economic development programs. A look at Table 4.3 will show that from 1961 to 1977 the developed world's financial assistance for fertility reduction efforts increased over fifty times, while its overall development assistance increased less than three times. Such data served to arouse the suspicions of many about the "true" reasons behind the developed world's support of fertility reduction efforts.

Table 4.3

Trends in Development and Population Assistance: 1961–1977

	Total Official Development Assistance[a]	Population Assistance[b]
	(in millions of U.S. dollars)	
1977	14,759	345[c]
1976	13,666	320
1975	13,588	287
1974	11,302	257
1973	9,400	182
1972	8,700	171
1971	7,700	155
1970	6,800	125
1969	6,600	86
1968	6,300	58
1967	6,600	30
1966	6,000	34
1965	5,900	18
1964	6,000	16
1963	5,800	11
1962	5,400	5
1961	5,200	6

[a]Excluding export credits, private investment, and other commercial transfers.
[b]Net totals excluding double-counting due to transfers between donors. Grants by voluntary organizations are not included for the years 1961–69. In 1970 these grants amounted to $0.9 million.
[c]Provisional.
Sources: Organization for Economic Co-operation and Development, governments, and annual reports of development assistance agencies and organizations.
Source: Jyoti Shankar Sigh, ed., World Population Policies *(New York: Praeger, 1979), Table 7.1 p. 206.*

Back in 1944, Frank Notestein had identified two patterns of socioeconomic/demographic change as being possible for the Third World: continuation of the existing agrarian society and a rise in mortality, or the transformation of agrarian societies into modern industrial ones and the eventual cessation of population growth through fertility decline.[20] Both these scenarios contained elements that were considered to be threatening to the interests of the United States and the West in general. If the first occurred and the less-developed world's population pressed against the available means of subsistence, then political and economic turmoil were likely consequences. The resulting catastrophes, Notestein argued, "would adversely affect the immediate economic interests of this country and of other Western powers that are heavily dependent on the specialized products of these regions."[21] If the second scenario occurred, then a "future world" would be created in which Western "peoples would become progressively smaller minorities, and possess a progressively smaller proportion of the world's wealth and power."[22]

The concern expressed by Third World states at Bucharest was that a global fertility reduction policy might constitute a key element of a third scenario of the future, a future that would see the cessation of population growth without seeing the transformation of agrarian societies into modern industrial ones. This scenario, unlike the two elaborated by Notestein, contained no threatening elements for the developed world. Without rapid population growth, stability in the Third World might be preserved. Without industrialization, the present global distribution of power and wealth also might be preserved. The slogan "development is the best contraceptive" was meant to highlight the concern of the Third World that fertility control efforts should not replace an emphasis on economic modernization.

SUMMARY AND CONCLUSION

During the last thirty years concern about rapid population has led many Third World nations to adopt fertility reduction policies. Although these nations do believe that a lowering of fertility will facilitate attaining national goals, controversy still surrounds the notion of a global application of birth limitation policies. The world is still divided into two major categories: the wealthier nations with low birthrates and the poorer nations with high fertility rates. It is believed that a divided world has divided interests. The major goal of the poorer nations is development —a movement out of poverty. Insofar as a national policy of fertility reduction proves to contribute toward achieving that end, then it will be pursued. But what is the major goal of the wealthier nations? Is it not stability, that is, "peace"? In pursuit of stability, the wealthier nations have advocated fertility reduction for the poorer nations. This advocacy arouses the suspicions of the Third World because "stability" has many meanings. If the Third World comes to perceive pursuit of stability to mean attempting to preserve the present distribution of wealth and power among nations, a global fertility policy will never be adopted. A global fertility reduction policy will be possible only if the Third World can be convinced that pursuit of stability means recognition that all peoples must come to share prosperity.

EXERCISE 4.1

Governmental Policies

How do you feel about the government's taking the following actions? Place a check in the box that comes closest to your feelings:

	ACCEPTABLE	ACCEPTABLE IN CERTAIN CIRCUMSTANCES	UNACCEPTABLE
The government's requiring parents to see that their children are innoculated against polio and smallpox.	☐	☐	☐
The government's determining who is permitted to become a permanent resident of the country.	☐	☐	☐
The government's allowing parents a tax deduction for each minor child who still lives at home.	☐	☐	☐
The government's determining which of its citizens is permitted to leave the country.	☐	☐	☐
The government's requiring that all automobiles sold in the country contain seat belts.	☐	☐	☐
A government child support payment's being sent annually to all parents for each child still at home.	☐	☐	☐
Tax fund's being spent to fund medical research seeking a cure for cancer.	☐	☐	☐
The government's offering free land to those willing to settle in frontier areas.	☐	☐	☐
The government's requiring proof of knowledge about contraception before allowing couples to marry.	☐	☐	☐
The government's offering tax rebates to those willing to move into depressed urban neighborhoods.	☐	☐	☐

	ACCEPTABLE	ACCEPTABLE IN CERTAIN CIRCUMSTANCES	UNACCEPTABLE
The government's requiring that all sources of drinking water be inspected regularly for purity.	☐	☐	☐
The government's requiring individuals to obtain a permit before changing residences.	☐	☐	☐
The government's offering cash payments to married couples who promise to have only one child.	☐	☐	☐
Tax fund's being used to assure that all individuals, regardless of ability to pay, have access to medical care.	☐	☐	☐
The government's making it a crime, punishable by fine and forced sterilization, to have more than two children.	☐	☐	☐

1. Classify each of the preceding government actions as being a migration policy, a mortality policy, or a fertility policy. Place a "Mi," "Mo," or "F" next to each.
2. Note how you judged each type of population policy. Do your answers show any pattern? Did you generally find acceptable government intervention to control mortality? Migration? How about fertility?
3. If a pattern is evident in your answers, reflect on why this might be the case. Can you write a paragraph justifying your answers?

EXERCISE 4.2

The 1,000 Peso Fine[23]

The Philippine National Assembly was in an uproar late last year over a previously obscure bill that would have fined mothers for every child they produced above two. The bill, the brainstorm of Assemblyman Marcial Pimental, proposed that a mother with two surviving children be fined 100 pesos for the birth of her third child, with the escalation of 100 pesos in fines for each additional child produced.

In the case of parents with an income of 100,000 pesos a year or more, the bill called for a 1,000 peso fine.

The reaction? A verbal parliamentary donnybrook that ultimately involved President Marcos (who was quick to reiterate his government family planning program's commitment to human dignity and the World Population Plan of Action).

Pimental's bill is given scant chance of Assembly passage. But Pimental (who incidentally is the father of eight) feels determined. His legislation is the outgrowth of his alarm over Philippine population growth (2.5 percent a year in 1978), and a feeling that the country's population program, though it is due to spend $130 million from 1978 to 1982, simply is not getting enough response from the Philippine people.

QUESTIONS

1. What type of policy has been proposed in the Philippines to limit family size? What is its purpose?

2. The article indicates that there will be much opposition to the proposed bill. Why?

3. What do you think about such a policy for the Philippines?

Now read the article in its amended form:

The $1,350 Dollar Fine

The U.S. Senate was in an uproar late last year over a previously obscure bill that would have fined mothers for every child they produced above two. The bill, the brainstorm of Senator Mark Post, proposed that a mother with two surviving children be fined $1,350 for the birth of her third child, with an escalation of $1,350 for each additional child produced.

In the case of parents with an income of $50,000 a year or more, the bill called for a $13,500 fine.

The reaction? A verbal congressional donnybrook that ultimately involved President Reagan (who was quick to reiterate his government's commitment to human dignity and the World Population Plan of Action).

Post's bill is given scant chance for Senate passage. But Post (who incidentally is the father of four) feels determined. His legislation is the outgrowth of his alarm over American population growth (.6 percent a year).

QUESTIONS

1. Would there be as much opposition in the U.S. Congress as there appears to be in the Philippine Assembly? Would the bill pass the Senate?

2. What do you think about such a policy for the United States? Is it the same answer you gave for the Philippines? Why or why not?

3. Do you think you would support a bill such as the one outlined in the article? Do you think your parents would be likely to support it? Your friends?

NOTES

1. Dorothy Nortman and Ellen Hofstatter, *Population and Family Planning Programs,* 10 ed. (New York: Population Council, 1980), Table 20, pp. 68–69.

2. The following description of China's fertility reduction program came from three sources: Bernard Berelson and Jonathan Lieberson, "Government Efforts to Influence Fertility," *Population and Development Review,* 5, No. 4 (December 1979); Pi-chao Chen's introduction to Chen Muhua's "Birth Planning in China," *Family Planning Perspectives,* 11, No. 6 (November/December 1979); Nortman and Hofstatter, *op. cit.*

3. The description of Singapore's fertility reduction program comes from two sources: Berelson and Lieberson, *op. cit.,* and Nortman and Hofstatter, *op. cit.*

4. The description of India's fertility reduction program comes from the two sources mentioned in note 3.

5. The description of Indonesia's fertility reduction program comes from the two sources mentioned in note 3.

6. Berelson and Lieberson, *op. cit.,* p. 588.

7. The description of the Philippines' fertility reduction program comes from the sources mentioned in note 3.

8. Edward A. Ross, "Western Civilization and the Birthrate," *American Journal of Sociology,* 12, No. 5 (March 1907), p. 610.

9. Frank Notestein, "Population—The Long View," in *Food for the World,* edited by Theodore Schultz (Chicago: University of Chicago Press, 1945), pp. 51–52.

10. Chen Muhua, "China Sets Even More Stringent Targets of Fertility Reduction," *Population and Development Review,* 5, No. 4 (December 1979), p. 726. This article is an excerpt from one originally appearing in *Renmin Ribao* (People's Daily) on August 11, 1979.

11. See the review of such correlational studies contained in Julian Simon's *The Economics of Population Growth* (Princeton: Princeton University Press, 1977), pp. 139–140.

12. *Ibid.,* Chapter 3, and Simon Kuznets' *Modern Economic Growth* (New Haven: Yale University Press, 1966), Chapter 1.

13. The two "classic" studies are Ansley Coale and Edgar Hoover's *Population Growth and Economic Development in Low-Income Countries* (Princeton: Princeton University Press, 1958) and Stephen Enke's *Economics for Development* (New Jersey: Prentice-Hall, 1963).

14. This criticism is made by both Simon Kuznets and Gunnar Myrdal. See Kuznets, "Economic Aspects of Fertility Trends in the Less Developed Countries," in *Fertility and Family Planning,* edited by S. J. Behrman *et al.* (Ann Arbor: University of Michigan Press, 1969), p. 175; and Myrdal, *Asian Drama,* Vol. III (New York: Pantheon, 1968), pp. 2068–2075.

15. Harvey Leibenstein made this observation when reviewing the work of Stephen Enke. See Harvey Leibenstein, "Pitfalls in Benefit-Cost Analysis of Birth Prevention," *Population Studies,* Vol. 23, No. 2 (July 1969), pp. 161–170.

16. Frank Notestein, "The Population Council and the Demographic Crisis of the Less Developed World," *Demography,* 5, No. 2 (1968), p. 553.

17. Dwight D. Eisenhower, "Let's Be Honest with Ourselves," in *Saturday Evening Post,* Oct. 26, 1963, p. 27. Quoted in Phyllis Piotrow's *World Population Crisis* (New York: Praeger, 1973), p. 46.

18. Lyndon Johnson, "President Johnson's Message to Congress on Foreign Assistance," *Department of State Bulletin*, Vol. 54, No. 1392 (February 28, 1966), p. 321.

19. See Nortman and Hofstatter, *op. cit.*, Tables 6 and 10.

20. Frank Notestein, "Problems of Policy in Relation to Areas of Heavy Population Pressure," in Milbank Memorial Fund's *Demographic Studies of Selected Areas of Rapid Growth* (New York: Milbank Memorial Fund, 1944).

21. *Ibid.*, p. 155.

22. *Ibid.*, p. 156.

23. *Intercom*, 7, No. 2, p. 10.

chapter 5

THE FUTURE
OF POPULATION

In 1980, the best estimate of the world's population was approximately 4.4 billion people; it was increasing at about 1.8 percent annually.[1] Of course, such figures are educated guesses, since about one-half of the world's nations, containing even a larger share of the population, do not have fully reliable systems for collecting information on births and deaths—the vital events that change the size of the population in most nations. Where migration is also a major force, accurate information may be even more elusive. But we can take sufficient confidence in figures like 4.4 billion people to consider a future where growth rates of 1.8 percent will add 79 million each year.

It is the present, of course, that allows one to glimpse into the future. The likelihood of continued population growth is great, for this growth is aided by the large numbers of the recently born who will soon enter into their own reproductive years and will contribute to an increase in numbers even if they have fewer children than their parents did. Such prospects vary for the "economically developed" nations and those of the developing or Third World. In the immediate past— 1975–1980—the annual growth rate of the developing nations has been increasing at a rate more than three times as great as their more developed counterparts (2.21 percent *vs.* 0.67 percent). The major reason for this difference is higher fertility: a birthrate of 33.6 per 1,000 for the Third World versus 15.6 per 1,000 for the developed world. At the same time, the crude death rates are rapidly becoming similar. Hence, the prospects for future growth in the developing countries, based upon the differences in fertility and the social, cultural, and economic change that would have to be implemented to narrow them, are indeed significant. Today three of every four of the world's people live in the Third World. But it is evident that this proportion promises to widen, a change that has a profound impact upon the economic, political, and social relationships among the various nations.

Grouping population statistics both conveniently summarizes demographic patterns and also obscures differences among the nations in the developed and the

109

developing worlds. In the developing world, the differences among the nations are noteworthy. To illustrate, one can compare the annual rates of population increase. East Asia has an annual rate that is less than one-half of that for Africa (1.32 percent and 2.91 percent respectively). And in South America, the growth rates for the tropical and temperate regions also differ greatly. These differences have been discussed elsewhere in this volume; here they serve as reminders of the different demographic experiences (and contributing forces) that are present in various nations and as possible clues to the future course of population growth throughout the world. Since there is usually an inverse relationship between a nation's level of socioeconomic development and its demographic growth—the better the socioeconomic situation, the lower the growth rate—the differences within the group of economically developing nations, with quite different patterns of development, should be most instructive.

THE ART OF PROJECTING THE FUTURE

Future trends in population growth are predicted, then, by taking a good look at the present. But it is also necessary to ask some hard questions about the prospects for conditions that govern the present remaining the same in the future. If there appears to be little prospect for change, the forecast becomes a simple extrapolation of current rates into the future. But if conditions are likely to change, adjustments need to be made. The forecaster needs to judge what should happen. Although the methodology of projecting the course of population growth into the future is somewhat involved and technical, the accuracy of the final outcome really depends on how accurate the forecaster's guesses and assumptions are.

There are a number of different ways of making such projections, but most projections have been made by using the *component method*. In this approach population growth is broken down into its component parts—fertility, mortality, and migration. Here, we return to the demographic equation that incorporates these components:

$$P^{now} = P^{then} + Births - Deaths \pm (In\text{-}Migration - Out\text{-}Migration)$$

Adjusted slightly for its new task of predicting the future, this equation becomes:

$$P^{future} = P^{now} + Births - Deaths \pm (In\text{-}Migration - Out\text{-}Migration)$$

In the component method, the process variables —fertility, mortality, migration— are each analyzed separately. Past trends in fertility and mortality are examined and assumptions are then made about future levels in these two vital processes. Generally, sets of age-specific fertility rates and probabilities of survival (a reflection of mortality) are specified for each five-year period for the next twenty or thirty years. To organize the information, forecasters work with five-year age groupings (called cohorts) and look at their demographic experience (fertility and mortality) in the series of five-year sets.

Figures 5.1 and 5.2 suggest how the procedure operates. Figure 5.1 offers a

Figure 5.1

PROJECTING SURVIVORS BY THE COMPONENT METHOD

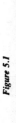

MALES

Projected Survivors (3)	Projected Survival Rates 1980–85 (2)
0 =	.000 ×
86.710 =	.667 ×
207.900 =	.770 ×
328.770 =	.843 ×
462.280 =	.889 ×
568.520 =	.932 ×
563.450 =	.955 ×
671.370 =	.973 ×
639.600 =	.984 ×
632.960 =	.989 ×
634.880 =	.992 ×
644.150 =	.991 ×
782.100 =	.990 ×
734.820 =	.993 ×
718.560 =	.998 ×
828.340 =	.998 ×
885.600 =	.984 ×

1980 Age-Sex Structure

Age	Males (1)	Females (1)
90		
85		
80	90,000	300,000
75	130,000	310,000
70	270,000	430,000
65	390,000	530,000
60	520,000	620,000
55	610,000	660,000
50	590,000	620,000
45	690,000	690,000
40	650,000	630,000
35	640,000	620,000
30	640,000	600,000
25	650,000	620,000
20	790,000	760,000
15	740,000	670,000
10	720,000	660,000
5	830,000	750,000
	900,000	810,000

Population in 100,000s

9 8 7 6 5 4 3 2 1 0 1 2 3 4 5 6 7 8 9

FEMALES

Projected Survival Rates 1980–85 (2)	Projected Survivors (3)
.000 =	0
.794 =	246,140
.877 =	377,110
.898 =	475,940
.922 =	571,640
.944 =	623,040
.965 =	598,300
.977 =	674,130
.985 =	620,550
.991 =	614,420
.994 =	596,400
.996 =	617,520
.997 =	757,720
.997 =	667,990
.997 =	658,020
.998 =	748,500
.987 =	799,470

STEP ONE: Compile the most current age-sex information (Column 1).

STEP TWO: Analyze past mortality trends and derive the set of age-specific survival rates that you feel will hold for the next five years (Column 2).

STEP THREE: Calculate the projected number of survivors by age and sex five years hence (Column 3) by multiplying Column 1 by Column 2.

Figure 5.2

PROJECTING BIRTHS BY THE COMPONENT METHOD

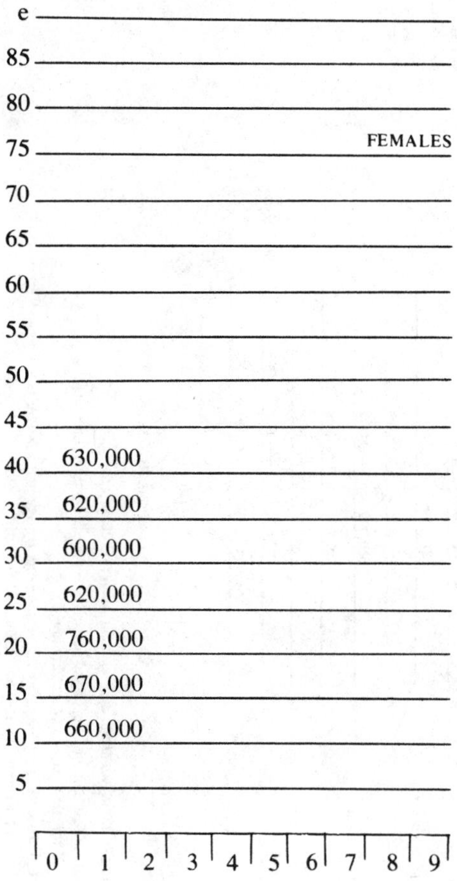

Women of Reproductive Age 1980 (1)	Projected Age Specific Fertility Rates 1980–85 (2)	Projected Births 1980–85 (3)
e		
85		
80		
75 FEMALES		
70		
65		
60		
55		
50		
45		
40 630,000	× .025 =	15,750
35 620,000	× .110 =	68,200
30 600,000	× .280 =	168,000
25 620,000	× .570 =	353,400
20 760,000	× .605 =	459,800
15 670,000	× .300 =	201,000
10 660,000	× .005 =	3,300
5		1,269,450 Total Births Projected for 1980–1985.

```
0   1   2   3   4   5   6   7   8   9
```

STEP ONE: Compile information on the number of women of reproductive age (Column 1).

STEP TWO: Analyze past fertility trends and derive the set of age-specific fertility rates that you feel will hold for the next five years (Column 2).

STEP THREE: Calculate the projected number of births for the five-year period by multiplying Column 1 by Column 2.

112

graphic presentation of how survivors are projected from 1980 to 1985. It begins with a schedule of specific probabilities of survival for males and females by age (five-year groups). The technicalities of identifying these probabilities need not concern us here, but they reflect the assumptions being made about the course of mortality in the five-year period. These probabilities for survival are applied to the current population, organized by age and sex, and these calculations provide the number of survivors in 1985.

It is then necessary to add the new persons who will join these survivors through their births during the period under consideration. The procedure is basically the same. A set of age-specific fertility rates, reflecting the assumptions being made, is applied to the number of females in each reproductive age group (14−45) to offer a projected number of births. Figure 5.2 offers a graphic presentation of the procedure.

Finally, the number of net migrants is estimated for the period and incorporated into the projected figures. Here, the technicalities of projections represent more of an art form. But with the information on all of the demographic processes in place, an age-sex structure is constructed and the whole procedure is repeated with this new population for the next five years with a new set of birthrates, survival probabilities, and estimates of migration. The procedure is repeated until the end of the period for making projections is reached.

It has become common to employ not one set of assumptions about the future course of fertility and mortality, but three. In addition to projecting the most likely demographic future (generally labeled the "medium variant"), projections are also made of the "high variant" and the "low variant." These are meant to represent the upper and lower limits of possible change. The high variant is the population size that will result from the highest plausible rate of fertility and the lowest plausible rate of mortality—a combination that produces the greatest growth. The low variant is the population size that will result from the lowest plausible fertility rate and the highest plausible mortality rate—a combination producing the least growth.

The use of two additional variants is not simply a face-saving action undertaken by timid demographers. The magnitude of the difference between the high and low variants does vary from one country to another and serves as a measure of the confidence that is placed in the medium variant. If the range is very large, the forecaster is saying that great faith should not be placed in the medium variant. If it is small, one can use the medium variant with more assurance.

Available World Population Projections

Currently, three major agencies generate world population projections: the United Nations, the World Bank, and the United States Bureau of the Census.[2] All use some form of the component method and all develop projections for each country as well as for major regions and the world as a whole. However, only the United Nations' projections take migration into account. Both the World Bank and the Bureau of the Census make the assumption that no international migration exists. This assumption does make the projections of certain nations' populations unrealistic, but of course, it does not affect the projections for the world as a whole.

Because the United Nations has the longest history of making world population projections (assessments were made in 1951, 1954, 1957, 1963, 1968, 1973, and 1978) and because of its ongoing efforts in this field, particular attention will be paid to its projections.

The real "art" of making population projections is not to be found in techniques used, the calculations made, or even in often ingenious methods devised to cope with problems of incomplete data. Any set of world population projections is technically correct if "correct" simply means that the figures projected accurately portray what would happen to population size, the growth rate, and the demographic structure under the mortality and fertility conditions that are assumed. The "art" of making projections rests on how one arrives at those assumed condtions.

Intuition, hunches arising from close scrutiny of recent trends, understanding of social and cultural changes and political conditions, sensitivity to changes in one nation that offer clues to the future in another—all these elements make up the real foundation of current projections. Demography does not yet provide any truly scientific way of predicting the future growth of population because there are no well-established models with which one can generate specific future developments from past trends. This is especially true of fertility. The figures contained in population projections flow from human judgments, not mathematical models or unchanging demographic laws. The accuracy of projections rests again on the quality of these judgments. Therefore, an examination of current projections must not simply be a consideration of the figures they contain, but it must also be an analysis of the judgments and data on which they are based.

FROM PAST TO PRESENT TO FUTURE

Comparing the past to the present is the starting point of all projections. The most recent series of world population projections use 1975 as the base date—the date at which an estimation of size is made and the date from which population figures are projected. In the near future, as more data become available, this base year will move to 1980. The year 2000 is the end date of the projection period. This time frame spanning a quarter century is then a convenient one to use. The recent past, 1950 to 1975, is the period that has been closely scrutinized for significant trends by those making the projections. And the judgments made about these trends serve as the foundation for the projected future. What then happened demographically from 1950 to 1975?

The Recent Past

In 1950 there were 2.5 billion people in the world. By 1975 an additional 1.5 billion had been added to arrive at a figure slightly over 4 billion. The population had grown at a rate approaching 2 percent a year. Historically, this was a period of growth without precedent. The world's population grew at a rate nearly four times the rate for the 19th century (.5 percent) and over two times the rate for the first half of the twentieth century (.8 percent). The demographic change that produced this unprecedented increase in human numbers was the dramatic reduction in mortality that swept the Third World. The world's population was "exploding" not from an increase in fertility but from unprecedented numbers of persons who were remaining alive longer. Between 1950 and 1975 over ten years were added to the life expectancies of men and women in the economically less developed world, with the crude death rate dropping by nine per 1,000. Even with the decline in fertility that occurred in many nations from 1950 to 1975, the growth rate crept higher because mortality declined much more rapidly than fertility.

In order to draw insights that might be useful for making population projections from the demographic trends of 1950–75, it is necessary to treat changes in mortality and fertility separately as they took place in the economically less developed nations and their more developed counterparts. The rate of growth and the future size of the world's population will be determined by the changes in the relationship between these two components throughout the world.

Mortality in the Third World

Mortality in the developing nations, whether measured by life expectancy or crude death rates, dropped remarkably during 1950–75. Is it likely to continue to decline at a similar rate from 1975 to 2000? One way to begin to answer this question is to examine what happened to the rate of decline in mortality over that twenty-five year period from 1950 to 1975.

Before beginning, however, a word must be said about measures of life expectancy at birth, which is the standard used extensively when studying mortality trends. Such figures are really a means to condense the mortality conditions existing among individuals of all ages at one time into a single number. It is not a prediction that any given individual will live a certain number of years. For example, life expectancy at birth for males in the United States in 1978 was 69.5 years. (Since males and females usually have quite distinct mortality patterns, it is common to calculate life expectancy separately for each sex.) This number was derived from analyzing the deaths that occurred among males of all ages in the United States during 1978. If a newborn baby boy experienced throughout his life the exact same chance of surviving from one birthday to the next that males of all ages experienced in 1978 (an unlikely occurrence), then he would live 69.5 years.

While having questionable utility as a predictive measure for individuals, this figure is an ideal comparative measure of mortality. One can directly compare the life expectancy figures of two nations and determine where the force of mortality is greater and by how much. One can directly compare the change in the life expectancy figures occurring within one area over time and determine the extent to which mortality conditions have improved. Life expectancy figures are not influenced by differences in age structure. For this reason, they are a much more accurate measure of mortality than crude death rates.

Please do Exercise 5.1: PROJECTING MORTALITY

Table 5.1 presents estimated life expectancy figures for the developing world. The apparent improvement shown in those figures for 1950 to 1975 shows a pattern. As can be seen by examining the male and female rates of increase in life expectancy, the earlier portion of that period saw more rapid mortality improvements than the latter portion. The five-year rate of increase was 7.6 percent at the beginning of the period, but it fell continuously throughout the period, and ended at a 4.0 percent level. The pace of mortality decline was slowing throughout the period.

In fact, the implementation of relatively inexpensive public health and disease control programs in many developing nations during the immediate postwar era brought a sudden and dramatic drop in death rates. Infectious diseases such as smallpox and endemic diseases such as malaria were quickly reduced during this time. The most dramatic improvements occurred at the youngest ages. In 1950 the infant mortality rate was over 200 deaths per 1,000 births in nearly all Third World countries. By 1975 this rate was well under 100 in many of these countries. Once the easily controlled diseases were reduced, however, the pace of mortality decline slackened as degenerative diseases, more difficult to control, rose in prominence as causes of death. By 1975 a number of areas of the Third World—much of Latin American, East Asia, Micronesia/Polynesia—had life expectancies beyond 60. Improvements in mortality conditions after this point are more difficult to accomplish, are more costly, and are likely to take more time.

Therefore, when making assumptions about the course of mortality in the Third World for the period 1975–2000, the makers of projections have forecast a less rapid mortality decline than occurred during the preceding twenty-five years. Table 5.2 contains projections for life expectancy in the Third World for 1975 to 2000. As shown in this table, male and female life expectancy is projected to move

Table 5.1

Estimated Third World Life Expectancy at Birth, Rates of Increase in Life Expectancy, 1950 to 1975

	1950– 1955	1955– 1960	1960– 1965	1965– 1970	1970– 1975
Male					
Life Expectancy	41.7	44.9	47.9	50.4	52.4
Rate of Increase in Life Expectancy	7.7%	6.7%	5.2%	4.0%	
Female					
Life Expectancy	43.5	46.8	49.8	52.4	54.5
Rate of Increase in Life Expectancy	7.6%	6.4%	5.2%	4.0%	

Source: World Population Trends and Prospects, By Country, 1950–2000: Summary Report of the 1978 Assessment (New York: Department of International Economic and Social Affairs, United Nations, 1979), Table 3-B. ST/ESA/ SER.R/33.

Table 5.2

Projected Third World Life Expectancy at Birth, Rates of Increase in Life Expectancy, 1975 to 2000

	1975– 1980	1980– 1985	1985– 1990	1990– 1995	1995– 2000
Male					
Life Expectancy	54.1	56.0	58.0	59.9	61.7
Rate of Increase in Life Expectancy	3.5%	3.6%	3.3%	3.0%	
Female					
Life Expectancy	56.2	58.2	60.4	62.3	64.5
Rate of Increase in Life Expectancy	3.6%	3.8%	3.1%	3.5%	

Source: World Population Trends and Prospects, By Country, 1950–2000: Summary Report of the 1978 Assessment (New York: Department of International Economic and Social Affairs, United Nations, 1979), Table 3-A. ST/ESA/ SER.R/33.

from the mid-50s range up past the 60 mark at modest rates, about 3+ percent every five years. Over the twenty-five-year period to the year 2000, life expectancy is projected to improve by 14 percent, compared to the 25 percent improvement that occurred between 1950 and 1975. The crude death rate is projected to fall 30 percent compared to the 41 percent drop for 1950–1975.

In general, the Third World regions that had the highest mortality in 1975, sub-Saharan Africa in particular, are projected to show the greatest decline during the next quarter century. Those areas that already had low mortality in 1975 are expected to show the lowest rate of mortality decline.

By the same token, the slackening of mortality decline predicted for the Third World should not be interpreted as implying that there is a growing danger of mortality increase in this region. There were mortality setbacks experienced in the 1970s by Bangladesh, due to political disturbances; by the Sahel region of sub-Saharan Africa, due to prolonged drought; and most recently by Cambodia, due to political upheaval. However, there is little evidence that any area of the Third World has experienced more than short-term increases in mortality. Both Bangladesh and the Sahel did experience rapid recoveries after the initial disasters. Substantial decline in mortality is now projected for both areas.

The correct interpretation to be given the projected slackening of the decline in mortality is that death control has progressed so quickly in the Third World that continued rapid gains in life expectancy cannot be reasonably expected. Many of the diseases and conditions that are "easy" to control have now been dealt with, leaving more challenging problems. By the year 2000, the Third World is projected to have life expectancy figures in the low 60s, quite similar to those of the developed world in 1950. This will be a remarkable achievement since no economist forecasts that the Third World will have attained a comparable level of economic development. One consequence of a slackening of the decline in mortality in the Third World is that it will also facilitate a decline in population growth.

Mortality in the Developed World

Mortality in the economically more developed world between 1950 and 1975 experienced some interesting trends which have significant implications for the future. As can be seen in Table 5.3, the period began with a male life expectancy of 63.1 years and a female life expectancy of 67.3, a male/female difference of 4.2 years. During this quarter of a century female life expectancy increased 7.5 years while the male figure increased only 4.5 years. The period ended with a male/female difference of 7.2 years. Thus, the differential had significantly increased. If five-year rates of change are examined in Table 5.3, the pattern of decline found in the Third World rates (see Table 5.1) is evidenced in an even more striking form in the developed world. The advances in life expectancy took place primarily prior to 1965, after which there was only slow improvement. It seems as though a ceiling might exist on life expectancy improvements which the developed world approached near the end of this period.

Further examination of mortality statistics tends to support this notion. The life expectancy figures among developed nations for the period 1950—55 show that a substantial range existed. The average female figure for the developed world was 67.3 years, but the figure for Norway was 74.5, while that of Yugoslavia was 60.3. A similar 15-year differential existed for male figures. By 1970—75 this range had been cut in half. The average male figure was 67.6 with a high of 72.1 years for Sweden and a low of 64.8 for Portugal; a similar 7-year range existed for female figures, although life expectancies were higher. Patterns within the developed world

Table 5.3

Estimated Developed World Life Expectancy at Birth, Rates of Increase in Life Expectancy, 1950 to 1975

	1950–1955	1955–1960	1960–1965	1965–1970	1970–1975
Male					
Life Expectancy	63.1	65.4	66.6	67.0	67.6
Rate of Increase in Life Expectancy		3.6%	1.8%	.6%	.9%
Female					
Life Expectancy	67.3	71.2	72.9	73.8	74.8
Rate of Increase in Life Expectancy		5.8%	2.4%	1.2%	1.4%

Source: World Population Trends and Prospects, By Country, 1950–2000: Summary Report of the 1978 Assessment (New York: Department of International Economic and Social Affairs, United Nations, 1979), Table 3-B. ST/ESA/ SER.R/33.

were converging. By 1970–75 the very clear relationship that had existed in 1950–55 between a country's socioeconomic level and its life expectancy had also become quite blurred. A level of mortality that is converging and becoming increasingly independent of socioeconomic factors seems to indicate that a life expectancy ceiling might exist.

These trends imply that great advances in life expectancy cannot be expected for the developed world for the period 1975 to 2000. As shown in Table 5.4, it is estimated that during this entire twenty-five-year period there will be an increase of only 1.8 years in the life expectancy of both males and females. An examination of the projected rate of increase in life expectancy contained in Table 5.4 shows about .6 percent improvement occurring every five years, a very low rate indeed for the twentieth century.

Heart disease, cancer, and strokes are already the three main causes of death in the economically developed world. These causes primarily affect the aged. Therefore, for substantial increases in life expectancy to result, major medical breakthroughs leading to their elimination would have to be made. Few other avenues for improving mortality conditions exist. Currently, deaths due to violence and accidents are far more numerous than those due to communicable diseases. Between 1950 and 1975, the infant mortality rates were halved in nearly every developed country. Except for some countries in Eastern and Southern Europe, very little room exists for further significant reduction in infant mortality.

Because the developed world is likely to experience both a very slow rate of improvement in life expectancy and a gradual "aging" of its population due to declining fertility, a curious phenomenon will take place in the crude death rate for this group of nations. It is likely that the rate will actually increase from 9.4 to 10.1 per 1,000 between 1975 and 2000. This increase will be in the opposite direction

Table 5.4

Projected Developed World Life Expectancy at Birth, Rates of Increase in Life Expectancy, 1975 to 2000

	1975– 1980	1980– 1985	1985– 1990	1990– 1995	1995– 2000
Male					
Life Expectancy	68.3	68.7	69.2	69.7	70.1
Rate of Increase in Life Expectancy	.6%	.7%	.7%	.6%	
Female					
Life Expectancy	75.5	76.0	76.5	76.9	77.3
Rate of Increase in Life Expectancy	.7%	.7%	.5%	.5%	

Source: World Population Trends and Prospects, By Country, 1950–2000: Summary Report of the 1978 Assessment (New York: Department of International Economic and Social Affairs, United Nations, 1979), Table 3-A. ST/ESA/ SER.R/33.

from that of actual mortality conditions, and, therefore, its utility as a measure of mortality will worsen. Already it is a very questionable mortality measure because it is so influenced by age composition. A number of Third World countries, because of their young populations, have lower crude death rates than those developed countries possessing significantly higher life expectancy figures. By 1995, the crude death rate of the Third World will be lower than that of the developed world.

Until recently, it had been common practice to use this rate for international comparisons because crude death rates were often the only measure of mortality available for a developing nation. This is no longer a sensible practice. The crude death rate, however, is still a measure of the annual rate at which people are being removed from the population by death. Since it will increase in the developed world, this sector's rate of population growth will correspondingly be reduced between 1975 and 2000.

> **Please do Exercise 5.2: LIFE EXPECTANCY INCREASES**

Fertility in the Developed World

The second component of population growth, fertility, has had a more volatile recent history than mortality, especially in the economically developed world. The period from 1950 to 1975 saw a "baby boom" followed by a "birth dearth" in a number of developed countries. Presently, these countries have rates of childbearing (see Table 5.5) that are at replacement level. What does the future hold? Will the developed world's fertility fall below replacement, will it stabilize at replacement level, or will an "echo" baby boom rebound throughout much of the region? Determining which scenario is most likely is exceedingly difficult. It must be remembered that no demographer studying the developed world's fertility in 1940 successfully predicted the postwar baby boom. Caution and tentativeness surround projections of the developed world's future fertility.

Table 5.5 presents the estimated and projected Gross Reproduction Rate (GRR) for the developed world and its constituent parts. This rate attempts to measure the relative size of successive generations of women. Once one becomes used to talking in terms of fractions of daughters, it is a very useful measure. A GRR of 1 implies that each woman, on the average, is bearing one daughter and thus is just "replacing" herself. A GRR of 2 (2 daughters) would imply a doubling in size from one generation to the next; a GRR below 1 implies a rate of childbearing below replacement. It must be noted that the GRR does not actually measure the average number of daughters a real generation of women has. It is a "synthetic" rate; that is, it presents the childbearing behavior of women of various ages during one calendar year as though one actual woman had behaved this way throughout her childbearing years. Because it is a synthetic rate, the GRR can change substantially over a short period of time—note the drop of almost half a daughter experienced by North American women between 1960−65 and 1965−70. But it is an excellent

Table 5.5

Gross Reproduction Rates, Estimated and Projected, for the Developed World, 1950–2000

Regions	Estimated[b]				Projected[a]					
	1950–1955	1955–1960	1960–1965	1965–1970	1970–1975	1975–1980	1980–1985	1985–1990	1990–1995	1995–2000
Developed World	1.41	1.38	1.35	1.21	1.11	.99	.98	1.00	1.02	1.04
North America	1.61	1.78	1.70	1.24	1.03	.89	.93	.97	1.00	1.00
Japan	1.46	1.05	.95	.99	1.04	.89	.85	.92	.96	.99
Eastern Europe	1.45	1.35	1.26	1.07	1.05	1.10	1.08	1.06	1.04	1.03
Northern Europe	1.15	1.24	1.35	1.27	1.09	.87	.86	.90	.96	1.02
Southern Europe	1.31	1.27	1.31	1.30	1.20	1.10	1.06	1.03	1.03	1.04
Western Europe	1.16	1.21	1.29	1.24	1.02	.80	.80	.83	.91	1.02
Australia–New Zealand	1.56	1.69	1.69	1.43	1.37	1.03	.98	.94	.95	.98
U.S.S.R.	1.45	1.38	1.26	1.18	1.17	1.16	1.15	1.15	1.14	1.14

[a]Source: World Population Trends and Prospects, By Country, 1950–2000: Summary Report of the 1978 Assessment (New York: Department of International Economic and Social Affairs, United Nations, 1979), Table 4. ST/ESA/SER.R/33

[b]Source: World Population Prospects as Assessed in 1973 (New York: Department of Economic and Social Affairs, United Nations, 1977), Tables 25, 38. ST/ESA/SER.A/60.

fertility measure to use for international comparisons because its value can be intuitively understood and, unlike the crude birthrate, it is not affected by differences in age structure.

What insights can be gained from examining trends in the Gross Reproduction Rate from 1950 to 1975? The first point to note is that the period 1970−75 shows a remarkable convergence of fertility levels within the developed world, at a level slightly above replacement. No longer do you find the wide differential that existed among the GRRs for nations of the developed regions for the period 1955−65. The immediate postwar era was a time of divergence in fertility trends. Some developed countries experienced a significant jump in GRRs: the "baby boom" of North America, Northern and Western Europe, Australia and New Zealand. Japan, Eastern and Southern Europe, and the U.S.S.R., however, experienced either stable GRR levels or significant declines. The sharp drop in the GRR that began after 1965 in those nations that had undergone the great increases of the baby boom produced a more uniform GRR pattern for the developed world by 1970−75.

Are there underlying reasons for this present uniformity or is it a temporary situation which will not last? Although this is a difficult question to answer, a case can be made for the significance of this present trend. A number of social changes have been experienced throughout the economically developed world that could be leading to a long period of low fertility. The rate of female participation in the labor force has been steadily increasing, leading to an improvement in the social status of women. The widespread experience of inflation has made the two-income family increasingly the norm, as the woman's earning power is needed to meet the rising costs of childbearing. Rising divorce rates throughout the developed world have also had a dampening effect on fertility. Improvement in contraceptive technology coupled with the general legalization of abortion have permitted improved fertility control to occur. None of these social trends shows signs of abating and all work to keep fertility low.

Therefore, when projecting the future course of fertility for the developed world (see the last five columns in Table 5.5), the assumption has been made that fertility will remain low and stablilize near a replacement GRR level of 1. It should be noted that a GRR of 1 does not mean that a population is currently experiencing a situation where births equal deaths; that depends on its particular age structure. It simply predicts that unless current age-specific birthrates change, such an equilibrium will occur in the future. For example, the most recent GRR of the U.S. is below 1, but the population continued to experience growth because the girls born during the postwar baby boom are now women of childbearing age and, although their fertility is low, births are more numerous than deaths since this group constitutes such a large proportion of the total population. So the population continues to grow. But as these women age, they will be replaced by fewer women in the fertile years and births will decline to the point where they would equal death if replacement levels of fertility continue.

Where fertility has been at a low level for a longer period, deaths are actually now more frequent than births and the rate of natural increase is negative. West Germany, East Germany, and Austria currently are in such a situation. If the fertility projections are correct, more developed countries are likely to join this group shortly. It is too early to tell if governments will be alarmed by this situation and implement pronatalist population policies. Nor can it be foretold whether such policies might be effective. Such action might eventually be necessary to keep fertility at replacement levels. It is possible that fertility projections of stability at replacement levels could turn out to be too high.

There are also demographers who predict an increase in fertility, particularly for those developed countries that experienced a postwar baby boom. This "echo" boom is predicted to begin in the late 1980s and 1990s when the smaller cohorts born after 1965 begin to enter the labor market. Because of their small size these cohorts might find their labor in greater demand, experience high starting salaries, marry earlier, and have more children. Such a scenario emphasizes the importance of economic contributions in determining fertility and disregards the importance of the social factors mentioned earlier.

The projection of stability at replacement levels, therefore, is a cautious one which stands between assuming a continuing fertility decline, on the one hand, or a possible fertility upturn for the developed world, on the other.

Fertility in the Third World

The future trend of fertility in the Third World, already inhabited by three out of every four persons on earth, will have a decisive impact on the size and growth rate of the world's population in the year 2000 and beyond. Are we at a turning point in Third World fertility? Has an era of rapid fertility decline begun? Unfortunately, when such important questions are asked concerning Third World fertility, the quality of the data is not fully adequate to provide appropriate answers.

Less than 10 percent of the Third World's population lives in countries possessing reliable vital registration systems. To calculate a Gross Reproduction Rate it is necessary to know not only the annual number of births but also the age of the mother at the time of birth. In many developing countries, no attempt is made to collect such information. As a consequence, analysis of recent fertility trends must be based on trends in the crude birthrate and that rate, as a measure of fertility, is not particularly appropriate for comparative or projective purposes. Moreover, even this elementary measure requires knowledge of the annual number of births and an accurate estimate of total population size. Unfortunately, such information is also of questionable accuracy for a significant portion of the Third World. Table 5.6 contains the best estimates of crude birthrates for the period 1950–75.

With these "best estimates," what trends can be uncovered? Between 1950–55 and 1970–75, there was a 15 percent decline in the Third World's birthrate. Seventy percent of this decline occurred during the last ten years. Not all regions participated equally in this trend. The birthrate for Africa declined very little and that for South Asia dropped only slightly more. Most of the Third World's aggregate decline was in fact due to the 35 percent drop in the Chinese birthrate. Nonetheless, East Asia (excluding China) as well as Latin America experienced noteworthy, although not equally substantial, declines.

When countries are examined instead of regions, areas of substantial decline can

Table 5.6

Estimated Third World Crude Birthrates, by Region, 1950 to 1975

Region	Estimated Crude Birthrate				
	1950–1955	1955–1960	1960–1965	1965–1970	1970–1975
Third World	41.8	41.6	40.0	37.7	35.5
Africa	48.1	48.0	47.6	46.9	46.1
Latin America	41.4	40.7	39.9	38.0	36.3
China	39.8	37.6	33.8	29.5	26.5
Other East Asia	36.6	41.7	38.3	32.9	30.1
South Asia	43.2	44.5	44.1	42.6	40.5

Source: *World Population Trends and Prospects, By Country, 1950–2000: Summary Report of the 1978 Assessment (New York: Department of International Economic and Social Affairs, United Nations, 1979), Table 2-B ST/ESA/ SER.R/33.*

be isolated still further. During the period 1950–75, 22 countries had a decline in their crude birthrates of more than 20 percent. Eight of these were island nations containing populations of less than one million. Seven were countries with populations of considerable size (over ten million): Chile, Colombia, Venezuela, China, South Korea, Malaysia, and Sri Lanka. Several additional larger countries had crude birthrate declines in the 16 to 18 percent range: Egypt, Thailand, and Turkey.

This trend, although it is obviously not present throughout all the Third World, does represent a historic breakthrough. Prior to 1950, there was little evidence anywhere in the Third World that fertility had fallen from its traditionally high levels. By 1975, a significant number of Third World countries—at different levels of economic development, in different geographic regions, and with different cultural heritages—had experienced marked fertility declines.

Since the declining trend is of quite recent origin, it is difficult to predict its probable pace, magnitude, or scope. However, the evidence that does exist suggests the trend might prove unprecedented with respect to each of these characteristics as well. In several cases the rate of this contemporary fertility decline can find no equal in the historic records of the now developed countries. For example, the crude birthrate of Singapore dropped from 44.4 in 1950–55 to 34.0 in 1960–65 to 21.2 in 1970–75; it was more than halved in 25 years. Costa Rica's birthrate fell over 30 percent in 10 years (45.3 in 1960–65 to 30.9 in 1970–75), while during the same period Hong Kong's rate fell over 40 percent (from 33.1 to 19.6). If the crude birthrate figure of 18.43 released by Chinese officials in 1979 is correct, then the Chinese birth rate has been almost cut in half in twenty years.

The crude birthrates below 20 noted above, indicate an extent of decline that is unprecedented. Such figures are as low as the crude birthrates of a number of developed countries: Ireland, Iceland, Australia, and New Zealand. There is also evidence that fertility decline is a trend that is spreading rapidly. Between 1965 and 1975, the crude birthrate fell noticeably not only in the twenty-five countries mentioned earlier but also in Indonesia, the Philippines, Cuba, the Dominican Republic, and Jamaica. Although it can be dangerous to make much of small changes occurring over short periods of time, these changes do suggest that this trend is expanding its range. Currently, about one-half of the population of the Third World resides in countries that have experienced an average annual 1 percent decline in fertility for the past 15 years. If India, Indonesia, the Philippines, and Mexico were to join this group in the near future, and evidence suggests that they might, this figure would increase to over two-thirds of the Third World.

How one answers questions concerning the possible pace, magnitude, and scope of this trend in the future determines the nature of the population projections one produces. The projected crude birthrates and gross reproduction rates contained in Table 5.7 are those of the latest U.N. projections. (Note that it is easy to project

Table 5.7

Projected Third World Crude Birthrates and Gross Reproduction Rates, by Region, 1975 to 2000

Region	Projected Fertility Measures				
	1975–1980	1980–1985	1985–1990	1990–1995	1995–2000
THIRD WORLD					
Crude Birthrate	33.6	32.1	30.6	28.3	26.2
Gross Repro. Rate	2.31	2.12	1.96	1.79	1.63
AFRICA					
Crude Birthrate	46.0	45.0	42.9	40.1	36.9
Gross Repro. Rate	3.13	3.06	2.90	2.68	2.41
LATIN AMERICA					
Crude Birthrate	35.4	34.4	33.0	31.3	29.6
Gross Repro. Rate	2.41	2.29	2.16	2.02	1.89
CHINA					
Crude Birthrate	22.1	20.1	19.7	18.0	17.4
Gross Repro. Rate	1.52	1.20	1.10	1.00	1.00
OTHER EAST ASIA					
Crude Birthrate	27.8	26.1	24.5	22.4	20.3
Gross Repro. Rate	1.84	1.57	1.40	1.29	1.20
SOUTH ASIA					
Crude Birthrate	38.9	36.9	34.1	31.0	27.8
Gross Repro. Rate	2.69	2.50	2.26	1.99	1.78

Source: World Population Trends and Prospects, By Country, 1950–2000: Summary Report of the 1978 Assessment (New York: Department of International Economic and Social Affairs, United Nations, 1979), Tables 2-A, 4. ST/ESA/SER.R/33.

GRRs for the Third World since the projection process uses age-specific birthrates that are simply assumed, not collected.) The major assumption underlying these projections is that fertility decline will eventually spread throughout the Third World. Socioeconomic and cultural factors may retard the onset of fertility decline and slow its pace in certain areas. Sub-Saharan Africa is a prime example. Active support for fertility reduction programs by governments is also assumed to have the effect of speeding up the process, as reflected in the greater projected decline for South Asia as compared to Latin America. A common course is assumed for all fertility transitions—decline will begin slowly, then speed up, and then slow down as low GRR levels are reached. It is assumed that the transition from high fertility to a replacement level (that is, a GRR of 1) will take only thirty years for some countries and as many as seventy years for other countries. Note that China is expected to have a GRR of 1 by 1990−95 while that for Africa in the year 2000 is still expected to be between 2 and 3.

The U.N. assumes that fertility decline will spread throughout the entire Third World by explicitly relying upon transition theory—"the latest United Nations projections are based essentially on the theory of demographic transition."[3] As noted earlier, transition theory argues that nations experiencing economic development will eventually experience a shift from high fertility to low fertility; this theory is based upon the historical experience of developed countries. Therefore, there is an implicit assumption in these projections that economic development will proceed throughout the Third World.

According to World Bank figures, annual rates of growth in Gross Domestic Product per capita have been significant for developing countries: 3.4 percent for 1960−70, 2.8 percent for 1970−80, and a projected 3.3 percent for 1980−90.[4] Therefore, there is some evidence supporting this implicit assumption. But it is important to note that assuming all countries will eventually attain replacement levels of fertility implies a world where all countries will eventually achieve significant levels of economic development. Questions concerning the plausibility of assuming universal attainment of replacement levels of fertility by the middle of the twenty-first century are difficult to address given our current state of knowledge.

By the year 2000, it will be known how accurate projections based upon such an assumption have turned out to be. The actual twenty-five-year set of projected fertility rates contained in Table 5.7 do seem to represent reasonable extensions of past trends. Between 1950 and 1975, the crude birthrate for the Third World fell 15 percent with most of the decline coming late in the period. Between 1975 and 2000, a 22 percent decline is projected, most of it occurring in countries where fertility has already started to decline. If one used as a benchmark the very extensive fertility declines that a number of countries have experienced over quite a short time period, projections of significantly more rapid fertility declines would result. Being properly inhibited by the very recent vintage of many countries' fertility decline and by the poor quality of much Third World fertility data, the United Nations has produced a more moderate set of fertility projections.

Please do Exercise 5.3: THE FUTURE DEPENDS ON YOU

International Migration

Migration, the third and final component of population growth, is the most difficult component to project. Statistics on international migration are deficient for both the developed and developing worlds. Both the direction and level of migration are often greatly influenced by political and economic trends of the moment. Therefore, for areas of the world where levels of net migration are small compared to the total population size, migration simply is not a component in the United Nations' projections. This is true for nearly all of Asia and Africa. Only when net migration flows are long-standing and likely to continue at a high level in the future do they enter into the population projections of countries. The flow from certain Latin American nations to North America and the flow from low-income populous Arab countries to high-income, sparsely settled Arab countries are prime examples of such cases. The projections of migration flows assume that they will be diminishing in strength by the turn of the century. This assumption does not have a firm empirical basis but simply reflects the difficulty of determining plausible net migration figures for the distant future.

PROJECTIONS OF POPULATION SIZE AND GROWTH

Having reviewed projected trends in the components of growth and the assumptions that underlie them, the population size and growth rate projections that result from these trends can now be examined. As is now clearly evident, these figures are simply the numerical consequences that result from applying the projected fertility, mortality, and migration rates to the known base population. Their accuracy will be determined by how closely reality conforms to assumptions made about the future course of fertility, mortality, and migration.

The World

As can be seen in Table 5.8, the world's population in the year 2000 is projected to be about 6.2 billion people. The last twenty-five years of this century will see more than two billion additional inhabitants on the planet, an increase close to the entire world's population as of 1950. In absolute terms, this increase will be the largest ever for a twenty-five-year period. The annual rate of increase will remain over 1.5 percent, a very high rate from any historical perspective.

When the direction of the rate of increase is examined, a continuous decline is noted. Between 1975 and 2000 the rate falls from 1.81 to 1.56, a drop of .25 of 1 percent. The decline is modest because both the crude birthrate and the crude death rate are expected to decline during the period, with the CBR dropping 2.5 points more than the CDR. This continuous, though modest, decline has great significance

Table 5.8

World Population Size and Rate of Increase Trends, 1950 to 2000

	World	
YEAR	POPULATION	RATE OF INCREASE (ANNUAL)
1950	2,513,000,000	
1955	2,745,000,000	1.77%
1960	3,027,000,000	1.95%
1965	3,344,000,000	1.99%
1970	3,678,000,000	1.90%
1975	4,033,000,000	1.84%
1980	4,415,000,000	1.81%
1985	4,830,000,000	1.80%
1990	5,275,000,000	1.76%
1995	5,733,000,000	1.66%
2000	6,199,000,000	1.56%

Source: World Population Trends and Prospects, By Country, 1950–2000: Summary Report of the 1978 Assessment (New York: Department of International Economic and Social Affairs, United Nations, 1979), Table 1. ST/ESA/SER.R/ 33.

for the world's population during the twenty-first century. The rate of decline for mortality will be slowing as world life expectancies pass 60. The rate of fertility decline is likely to remain steady or increase. If these assumptions hold true, the rate of increase in the world's population is likely to decline significantly during the early part of the next century. The world's rate of increase will have peaked in 1965 and then have begun a slow, but steadily increasing, decline. The last quarter of the twentieth century will be a time of large absolute increase in population size, largely because of the huge numbers in the childbearing years, but it may also be a historic turning point when the world's growth rate begins a clear downward course.

It is interesting that the latest United Nations projection (1978) has a lower world population size for the year 2000 than its predecessor (1973), which had a lower figure than its predecessor (1968). As the evidence accumulated concerning the extent of recent Third World fertility declines, projections of size and rates of increase had to be reduced.

The Third World and the Developed World

When the world is divided into developed and less-developed nations (see Table 5.9), the locus of future changes in population size can be clearly isolated. Between 1975 and 2000 the Third World's population will increase by nearly 2 billion people, the developed world's by only 179 million. Ninety-two percent of the population increase in the world will occur in the Third World. Throughout the period, its rate of increase will be over three times that of the developed world.

Because of the different growth patterns of the two sets of nations, the proportion

Table 5.9
Population Size and Rate of Increase Trends, Third World and Developed World—1950–2000

Population Size*

YEAR	THIRD WORLD	DEVELOPED WORLD
1950	1,681	832
1955	1,858	887
1960	2,082	945
1965	2,341	1,003
1970	2,628	1,050
1975	2,947	1,093
1980	3,284	1,131
1985	3,661	1,169
1990	4,069	1,206
1995	4,493	1,240
2000	4,926	1,272

Average Annual Rate of Increase

YEAR	THIRD WORLD	DEVELOPED WORLD
1950–1955	2.00%	1.28%
1955–1960	2.27%	1.27%
1960–1965	2.35%	1.19%
1965–1970	2.31%	0.91%
1970–1975	2.24%	0.81%
1975–1980	2.21%	0.67%
1980–1985	2.17%	0.67%
1985–1990	2.12%	0.62%
1990–1995	1.98%	0.56%
1995–2000	1.84%	0.51%

*in millions of people
Source: World Population Trends and Prospects, by Country, 1950–2000: Summary Report of the 1978 Assessment *(New York: Department of International Economic and Social Affairs, United Nations, 1979), Table 2. ST/ESA/ SER.R/33.*

of the world's population residing in the developed world will shrink from more than one-quarter to one-fifth. This assumes, of course, that there is no change in the composition of these two worlds. Perhaps by the year 2000, economic forces will have moved more nations into the category of developed, thereby dividing the world somewhat differently.

Major Regions

If the world is divided into eight major regions (see Table 5.10), we can gain an even more detailed understanding of future changes in size and rates of increase. Between 1975 and 2000, South Asia will increase in size by nearly one billion people, almost 44 percent of the entire world's population increase. Africa will increase by 422 million, East Asia by 343 million, and Latin America by 285 million. Changes in population size during this quarter century will be most dramatic in Africa, which will more than double its population, and Latin America, which will nearly do so. South Asia will increase by three-quarters, while East Asia will grow by only one-third. North America and the U.S.S.R. will increase by nearly a quarter, Europe by only one-tenth.

These different regional patterns of growth are a direct result of the markedly different rates of increase that will apply in various regions (see Table 5.10). The African rate of increase is the only one that will actually increase during this period, peaking in 1985, and it is also the highest, remaining close to 3 percent until 1990. Latin America's rate of increase will remain in the 2.5 percent range and experience only modest declines. But from a starting point well below 2 percent, the East Asian rate will experience sharp declines early in the period and be under 1 percent by 2000. The South Asian rate will experience sharp declines only in the last decades of the century and fall to slightly less than 2 percent by 2000. All the heavily populated developed regions will begin the period with rates of increase under 1 percent and by 2000 will have even lower rates, nearer the .5 percent range.

Countries

The projected changes in population size and rates of increase can also be analyzed for each country. The Appendix gives size and rate of growth projections for every country and area of the world. These country projections do forecast numerous significant alterations from the current situation. By the year 2000 the projected population of India (1.037 billion) will be approaching that of China (1.190 billion). During the last quarter of the twentieth century the populations of Mexico and Nigeria will increase by more than 120 percent and those of Brazil, Pakistan, and Bangladesh will double in size. In the year 2000, Brazil's population will be over 200 million, that of Bangladesh, Nigeria, and Pakistan around the 150 million mark, and that of Mexico over 130 million. A close scrutiny of these country projections will reward the examiner, especially when he or she remembers that these dramatic increases will occur within 25 years!

SUMMARY AND CONCLUSION

Obviously, the population projections examined here have implications far beyond the strictly demographic. For example, the changes in age structure projected for the Third world—more working people—should be beneficial to economic development efforts. The benefits will be significant, however, only if productive jobs can be found for the rapidly increasing numbers in the "productive ages." The absolute increase of nearly two billion people projected to occur in the

Table 5.10

Population Size and Rate of Increase Trends, Major Regions of the World, 1950 to 2000

Year	World	Africa	Latin America	Northern America	East Asia	South Asia	Europe	Oceania	U.S.S.R.
			POPULATION (MILLIONS)						
1950	2513	219	164	166	673	706	392	13	180
1955	2745	244	187	182	738	775	408	14	196
1960	3027	275	215	199	816	867	425	16	214
1965	3344	311	247	214	899	979	445	18	231
1970	3678	354	283	226	981	1111	460	19	244
1975	4033	406	323	236	1063	1255	474	21	254
1980	4415	469	368	246	1136	1422	484	23	267
1985	4830	545	421	258	1204	1606	492	24	280
1990	5275	630	478	270	1274	1803	501	26	292
1995	5733	726	541	281	1340	2005	510	28	302
2000	6199	828	608	290	1406	2205	520	30	312
			AVERAGE ANNUAL RATE OF INCREASE (PERCENTAGE)						
1950–1955	1.77	2.16	2.72	1.80	1.85	1.86	0.79	2.25	1.71
1955–1960	1.95	2.36	2.78	1.78	1.99	2.24	0.84	2.18	1.77
1960–1965	1.99	2.49	2.77	1.50	1.94	2.44	0.90	2.09	1.49
1965–1970	1.90	2.61	2.67	1.11	1.75	2.52	0.66	1.96	1.09
1970–1975	1.84	2.71	2.64	0.87	1.62	2.45	0.61	1.82	0.84
1975–1980	1.81	2.91	2.66	0.83	1.32	2.49	0.39	1.47	0.94
1980–1985	1.80	2.97	2.65	0.96	1.16	2.44	0.36	1.41	0.94
1985–1990	1.76	2.93	2.58	0.91	1.14	2.31	0.35	1.37	0.85
1990–1995	1.66	2.81	2.46	0.76	1.01	2.13	0.37	1.30	0.70
1995–2000	1.56	2.64	2.34	0.61	0.95	1.91	0.38	1.19	0.64

Source: World Population Trends and Prospects, By Country, 1950–2000: Summary Report of the 1978 Assessment (New York: Department of International Economic and Social Affairs, United Nations, 1979), Table 4. ST/ESA/SER.R/33.

Third World during the remainder of this century has clear implications for those concerned with the future demand for food, shelter, employment, and energy. The supply of these items will obviously have to increase in a correspondingly dramatic way if living standards are simply to remain constant. If development is to occur and if living standards are to rise, this increase has to be dramatically more substantive than that of population.

Food, energy, development, and population are all issues whose futures are intertwined. If food production falters, mortality is likely to increase and the population of the year 2000 is likely to be smaller than the projection of 6.199 billion. If rising energy costs cause development efforts to falter, Third World fertility may halt its decline and the population of the year 2000 may be much beyond 6.199 billion. The population projections just examined assume a future with development continuing in the Third World and with no mass starvation. For the future to be one worth living, let us hope that these assumptions and the optimistic future that they promise are correct.

EXERCISE 5.1

Projecting Mortality

Table A: Life Expectancy at Birth for the Third World, 1950−1975

	1950−55	1955−60	1960−65	1965−70	1970−75
Male	41.7	44.9	47.9	50.4	52.4
Female	43.5	46.8	49.8	52.4	54.5

1. Using the data contained in Table A, calculate the rate at which life expectancy figures increased from one five-year period to the next.
   Example: In 1955−60 male life expectancy was 44.9 years. In 1950−55 it had been 41.7 years. Between 1950−55 and 1955−60 male life expectancy increased 3.2 years. (44.9 - 41.7 = 3.2). The quinquennial (five-year) rate of increase in life expectancy was 7.7 percent (3.2 ÷ 41.7 = 7.6738 percent).

Quinquennial Rate of Increase in
Life Expectancy

	MALE	FEMALE
1950−55 to 1955−60	7.7%	_____
1955−60 to 1960−65	_____	_____
1960−65 to 1965−70	_____	_____
1965−70 to 1970−75	_____	_____

2. Write a paragraph analyzing what happened to the quinquennial rate of increase in life expectancy for the period from 1950 to 1975. Did the percentages increase over time? Did they decrease over time? Was there no pattern to their movement over time? If there was a pattern can you think of any reasons why this trend might have occurred?

3. Write a paragraph "projecting" the future trend of Third World mortality for the period from 1975 to 2000. Relate the *reasons* behind your projection.

EXERCISE 5.2

Huge increases in life expectancy ahead? The possibility of dramatically extending the human life span has been raised by the work of University of Wyoming scientist Joan Smith-Sonnenborn. By bathing common single-celled organisms in varying doses of ultraviolet light—first a dose to damage the cells and hasten the aging process, then radiation of a different wavelength to activate a photoreactive enzyme that is the cell's repair mechanism—she found that the treated cells showed a greater life span. The treated cells also showed a more youthful response to further radiation treatment, and when rounds of ultraviolet treatment were continued, a 50 percent increase in cell longevity resulted.[5]

QUESTIONS

1. What implication does Dr. Smith-Sonneborn's work have for the life expectancy of humans?

2. If, as a result of such research, people were able to live 50 percent longer than they do now, what would happen to the structure of existing populations? What might a changed age structure do to the economic situation of a country? to the social situation of a country?

3. On a purely demographic level, what would happen to mortality rates (survivorship rates)? to fertility rates? to growth rates?

4. How would Dr. Smith-Sonneborn's discovery affect population projections made prior to her research? after her research?

5. What do your answers to the above questions imply about the accuracy of population projections?

EXERCISE 5.3

The Future Depends on You

I. Fill out the following questionnaire:

Do you expect to marry at some time in your life? _____

   if yes, at approximately what age? _____
Do you expect to have children?
   if yes, _____
how many _____

at approximately what age will you have your first? _____

at approximately what age will you have your last? _____

approximately how long will you wait between children? _____

II. Look over your answers to the questionnaire and answer the following questions according to your own personal fertility projections:
1. Did you expect to marry? Why or why not?

2. What assumptions did you make when predicting your future fertility? How firm are those assumptions?
3. What if your assumptions turn out to be incorrect, how will that affect your fertility?
4. Were your assumptions based on social, political, or economic factors? Which factors were the most important?
5. Do you expect to have fewer, more, or the same number of children as there are in your own family? Suppose everyone chose to do as you have chosen, how would that affect world fertility?
6. Based on your own answers, what projections would you make about fertility in the next 25 years? What would your projections mean for the population structure of this country? the world?

NOTES

1. These figures are contained in the United Nations' most recent analysis of world population trends and prospects: *World Population Trends and Prospects, By Country, 1950−2000: Summary Report of the 1978 Assessment* (New York: Department of International Economic and Social Affairs, United Nations, 1979). ST/ESA/SER.R/33. Unless otherwise noted, all the demographic data contained in this chapter come from this report.
2. The most recent U.N. set of projections is the one cited in footnote 1. The U.S. Bureau of the Census set of projections is published in the Special Studies Series of the Current Population Reports: *Illustrative Projections of World Population to the 21st Century; Special Studies Series P-23, No. 79* (Washington, D.C.: Department of Commerce, 1979). The World Bank set of projections was prepared by K.C. Zachariah and My Thi Vu, *Stationary Population* (New York: World Bank, Population and Human Resources Division, 1978). The medium variants of all three sets of projections are remarkably alike. The world population size for the year 2000 is projected to be 6.199 billion (U.N.), 6.350 billion (Bureau of the Census), 6.054 billion (World Bank). There is only a 2 percent variance from the mean among these projections and the U.N.'s is right at that mean. This was an additional reason for selecting the U.N.'s projections for special analysis.
3. United Nations, *Prospects of Population: Methodology and Assumptions* (New York: United Nations, 1979), p. 28.ST/ESA/SER.A/67.
4. World Bank, *World Development Report, 1979* (Washington, D.C.: World Bank, 1979), Table 13, p. 13.
5. *Intercom*, Vol. 7, No. 4, p. 6.

chapter 6

THE "POPULATION PROBLEM" REVISITED

The great problem with the understanding of population dynamics is that they appear to be simple and familiar processes. And, for individuals, they are. But to effect change at societal levels in the population variables of fertility, mortality, and migration—if, indeed, change represents a proper goal—we need to appreciate the great complexity of this issue. As we have indicated, the conventional wisdom about population has been the starting point for analysis. Every informed citizen has heard about "the population problem" expressed in the figurative language of our times: "the Population Bomb," "the population explosion," and "lifeboat ethics." Rapid population growth represents a threat that is simple to understand. Appropriately, therefore, the solutions should also be simple. If there are too many people, then growth should be checked. But in advancing such arithmetically logical solutions, it is easy to ignore how awesome the task may be, especially given the momentum imparted by past increases, or how powerful are the values that support reproductive behavior and other demographic actions.

In the 1960s, some persons who were concerned with rapid population growth in the United States, as reflected in the baby boom that occurred after World War II, sponsored a series of newspaper advertisements to suggest the linkages that existed between population increases and various social ills in the United States. A typical advertisement pictured an older man, battered, with eyeglasses askew, who had obviously been a victim of a mugging. Aided by a text that blamed the crime rate on a growing population, the reader quickly made the desired connection. The evocative images of street crime and those who prey on the aged and others who are vulnerable were very helpful. The exact linkage might have been unclear but few were really concerned with the niceties of scientific causality.

Today, population growth in the United States has slowed and many large cities have declining populations. The advertisements linking crime to population growth no longer appear, but the newspapers remain full of accounts of muggings and other indignities perpetrated on the residents of urban areas, especially the aged. The connection between crime and population growth, if it exists, must then be more complicated than it was portrayed. At the very least, it may involve basic questions about social order. This is not to say that demographic factors, including shifts in the age composition, did not play an important role, especially as the babies born in the boom years moved into adolescence and young adulthood—the ages of most criminal activity. But a simple demographic interpretation of deviant behavior is clearly inadequate.

When we move from such an example of complexity to consider population as a global issue—especially the rapid growth that characterizes the Third World—the same kind of imagery and understandings of the issue become important. How do you portray population growth in a way that both raises people's consciousness *and* reflects population dynamics correctly and responsibly? Once again, the problem stems from the fact that the most dramatic images are not necessarily the most accurate ones. The pictures of starving children in Third World nations provide powerful impact (and identify a major tragedy), but do they really demonstrate population dynamics properly? The photographs of barrios, favelas, and shantytowns suggest the desperation of life in the crowded cities of the Third World, but do they accurately reflect demographic forces and issues?

The difficulties occur because these portrayals, when used to convey impressions about the crisis of population growth, as they often are, ignore other variables that can be very influential. The most terrifying photographs of starving children are taken in refugee camps; they testify more to the consequences of political conflict than to the imbalance between population growth and resources. The pictures of urban slums in Africa, Asia, and South America represent the outcome of the efforts of large cities to adjust to the influx of migrants, but they also disguise how people use such housing. Some slums contain persons who are desperately poor—the usual stereotype—but others provide shelter to those who are minimizing their housing costs to maximize other values. There are "slums of hope" in which residents have futures and "slums of despair" where prospects are bleak. Hence, even though the impact of marginal housing in the developing world challenges the sensibilities of middle-class Americans, it does not always reflect social and demographic realities accurately. It is important to avoid one-dimensional understandings in which important concerns are oversimplified.

The problem of representing concerns about population to the general public involves more than images. Most demographic processes are slow, determined, and virtually imperceptible, at least from day to day. To use a geological analogy, some issues are volcanic, others are glacial. From a newscaster's vantage point, or even that of a concerned analyst, the eruption of a Mount St. Helens may be more worthy of attention than the shifting of the Arctic ice cap (although the latter might attract some attention were it to grind over downtown Montreal). Volcanic processes are dramatic, powerful, and easy to portray. Glacial processes are slow and difficult to perceive, but relentless. And so, by analogy, population concerns are usually glacial. The sudden mortality in an epidemic or the dramatic influx of migrants into a community are exceptions that suggest how little notice persons usually take of demographic changes. Even the aggregate data that suggest how much populations have increased over a decade often come as a surprise, because the new additions through fertility or migration are spread over both time and space. Schools may be more crowded and waiting lines longer, but the changes are usually quite gradual. How then does one properly depict such developments to a general public?

The connection between population growth and growing malnutrition is as important as starvation through famine, however dramatic and tragic the latter cases may be. The association between population growth and unemployment and underemployment is also as important as the possible contributions of overcrowded conditions to street politics. But the imagery of the malnourished or unemployed has markedly less impact than that of starving children or riots. So, as we focus on dramatic cases, the results of demographic change may be improperly conveyed.

There is one additional issue. Not only do we need to deal with the powerful, though distorted representations about population growth, we need also to consider those who advance such news with a certitude that may be misplaced. By whose standards do we judge the impact of population growth and the importance of making changes in the pace of demographic change in the Third World? Whose interests are protected? Who has the right to suggest what solutions, and to whom?

The responses to these questions may not be the same from those in the economically developing nations and those in economically developed countries. Not only are the realities of population quite different—ranging from rapid growth in some Third World nations to the threat of declining populations in some nations of Eastern and Western Europe—but the history of demographic change and the character of contemporary politics are dramatically different. Many persons in nations that have both completed their demographic transition and made a similar transformation in economic development recommend that those in developing nations, and the rest of the world's populace, might be better served if growth rates were cut sharply in the Third World. But do not such arguments convey the clear suspicion, especially in those nations to which they are directed, that those nations which advocate them are really speaking from self-interest? Having accomplished their demographic transition and process of development, in large part with the resources extracted from the Third World through a variety of exploitative political and economic mechanisms, those who recommend or prescribe population control might be seeking simply to protect their present advantage. The truth, of course, is always elusive in complex matters, but things that are perceived as real can be real in their consequences. So, perceptions and images do matter.

It is clear, then, that we need to move beyond the convenient and simple approaches to population and not to judge knowledge about population growth and other changes by what appears superficially to make sense or fit our values. We need to "complicate" the subject, not simplify it, and place population matters, especially the rapid growth of the Third World, in proper balance. In this volume, we have used four perspectives to accomplish this task: *actors, values, policies,* and *futures*.

ACTORS

The first of the perspectives involves the actors in the population drama. We all play key roles in this production where the behavior of the chorus is especially important. As we have said repeatedly, demographic trends are the result of the combined decisions of many millions of individuals, couples, and families. Commonly held values and aspirations operate as a script that most of the population actors follow. But changes in that script require more than strokes of a pen; they require important social, economic, and cultural transformations. This is especially important because the cast is so large and efforts to change the rate of population growth must eventually influence the decisions and behavior of many millions of couples if they are to be successful. In nations where population growth is perceived as too low, reasons need to be provided for the actors to change their reproductive behavior and have more children. In the Third World, where most of our attention has been focused, the growth rates are high and the actors need to adopt a smaller family size as their ideal. And, to do so, they must adopt other values supportive of lower fertility. In the end, the drama would be a new one, quite contradictory to cultural tradition, and therefore uncertain of success.

To overwork the metaphor, this drama, or perhaps a musical or a light opera, has some actors with more important speaking parts, and others who are simply members of the chorus. But here we can never forget that the behavior of those millions in the population chorus is the raison d'être for the performance. Chapter 2 provides information on the emergence of those organizations and other institutional actors that seek stardom by influencing the performance of others. Since the cast is so large, they seek to accomplish this goal by influencing nations to accept their ideas so that, in turn, those whom they represent may adopt new goals and patterns of behavior. Since consensus on these goals is not established, the influences come from both the pronatalist and antinatalist "networks." Chapter 2 provides a program by which to identify the actors. It also suggests why the drama is beyond the resources of a community theater group. There are too many actors, many of whom want to star or at least control others, and the script is too complicated to follow easily. The key performers speak in different languages, both figuratively and literally, and they view the world in different ways. But at the very least, anyone who has tried to follow the script will never again think of the population drama in simple or conventional terms.

VALUES

A second major perspective to view population in a global context concerns values. As suggested, the trends and patterns in fertility and other forms of demographic activity are the result of the actions of thousands upon thousands of individuals or couples who act in similar ways. Thus, in a nation in which the average number of children per family might be three, some couples will have no children, others may have one, five, or more; but the great majority will have two, three, or four—a rather narrow range of reproductive behavior. The choices are narrowed not by specific directives, but by the adherence throughout the society and its culture to a common set of values. These values are often invisible and unspoken, but they are very powerful guides to human behavior.

Think about your own preferences for having children. It is unlikely that your notion of an ideal family size will differ greatly from those of your peers. Moreover, this is a decision that you have probably reached not through direct guidance or instruction by others, but rather quite automatically or unconsciously as shaped by powerful cultural expectations. This, of course, is one of the great difficulties faced in trying to develop family planning programs in developing nations. Even where the government or a private organization may have different goals for reproductive behavior, persons determine their own preferences for the number of children that are appropriate for a couple, and, when taken together, for a society. These preferences are embedded in the culture. The task, then, becomes to change the values upon which such choices rest. And that is a major undertaking.

Normally, persons pay little attention to the values that shape their own behavior. They are virtually automatic and unconscious. Issues emerge when values are challenged. This has very clearly happened in the case of population, especially matters of reproductive behavior. They represent problems of a very recent vintage.

The values that prevail in the case of population have remained unquestioned through most of human history. There was basically a pronatalist consensus derived from values that were supportive of population growth. Families sought large numbers of children; governments, if they played any role at all, were supportive of growth. Such attitudes were quite logical. Both families and societies needed to replace the losses caused by high mortality. Open frontiers and land to be occupied were incentives to increased numbers, through either fertility or immigration.

A major change occurred when mortality began to decline sharply while fertility remained high. The resulting rapid growth of the demographic transition generated pressures that caused the basic values underlying reproductive behavior to be questioned. Indeed, in the nations where the complete demographic transition has taken place and a new balance has been struck between low fertility and low mortality, a major shift in values occurred. The fact that transitions have occurred unevenly, leaving major differences between the economically developed and economically developing nations, has caused population to become an issue. The issue is therefore the consequence of two factors: the pressure of high growth and the economic differential that exists between two groups of nations.

There is a major distinction, however, between the pressure placed upon the values that supported reproductive behavior during the demographic transition of the developed nations, extending over two centuries, and the current pattern of fertility and mortality in the economically less developed nations. In the first instance, the changes in values were almost evolutionary. The shift in the vital rates was comparatively slow and societies and cultures could adjust and react. The frontiers were open—the New World for the entire nation and the beckoning economies of growing cities for rural areas—if any mistakes were made. Today, the situation is much more urgent: population growth has itself become more pressing;

the safety valves of the frontier and economies in need of labor are absent; and the differences between nations encourage some to try to impose or at least to suggest values for others.

In place of the common set of values supporting high fertility throughout most of human history, various societies and their supporting cultures define appropriate patterns of demographic behavior, especially reproductive patterns, in different ways. Equally important are the substantial differences in these nations in socioeconomic status, in race and ethnicity, and in other areas of consequence. For many nations, the differential growth, supported by clearly distinct cultural values, is a major problem and a challenge to uniform national policies.

Thus, assessment of the values that support demographic behavior, especially in matters of reproduction, must consider the world as a mosaic where the pieces vary. There are differing perceptions of the seriousness of the problem; differing assessments of the exact contribution of population growth and other demographic patterns to societal ills and their relationships to economic and social development; differing judgments about the appropriateness of the government's interest in a basic human activity (and the prevailing values which may or may not support that interest); and differing determinations of the correct response based on that view (for example, coercion *versus* voluntarism). Chapter 3 specifies the dimensions of these values and the complexity of the mosaic. But it also implicitly questions the aptness of the metaphor, because a mosaic is a pattern of pieces that fit closely together. Values are more often matters that set people apart. This observation is especially true for concerns about population growth in the contemporary world.

It is essential that we understand the differences in values about population behavior that do exist, especially attitudes toward family size. Within nations, differences by socioeconomic status, race, religion, and ethnicity are consistently found, and underscore the general differences in values that occur as a consequence of such variables. And those differences do matter. In Israel, for example, the higher fertility of the Arab population threatens to change the numerical balance with the Jewish population. Such concerns become political realities in other nations as well. It is a short step from awareness of such differences to prescriptions through policy. Similar patterns exist between nations. Therefore, when concern about the policies (or lack of policies) of nations toward population growth is expressed from without, it is directed to those values upon which demographic behavior and related policies are based. Prescriptions, then, address not superficial concerns, but rather the most basic ways by which couples look at the world. Usually, determinants of family size are fully consistent with commonly held cultural values and even if the numbers come up higher than those that others feel are appropriate, they are rational and consistent. They fit the culture. When people say "I cannot understand how they can have so many children," they are absolutely correct. They cannot, unless they understand the values that determine such behavior. The clear lesson here is that values are not wrong, merely different.

This is the reason why an understanding of values is so important. It moves us far beyond the notion that there is a prevailing and accepted code that is right. A careful look at values makes it clear that they fit the cultures in which they operate. They can change, but, because they are so fundamental and ingrained, such change takes time. So, urgency about population growth directly conflicts with the persistence of values and the consequent pace of change. Impatience in the face of this engenders imposed solutions that are more authoritarian and tend to ignore these values. But, in turn, such approaches require a detailed set of supporting values concerning coercion, freedom, and authority.

POLICIES

Values associated with demographic behavior are now often translated into population policies as one actor or set of actors attempts to influence the actions of others. Programs to curtail immigration or direct its course, those to influence couples to reduce fertility or to have more children, and efforts to eliminate disease and premature death are examples of policies that attempt to manipulate the demographic process variables. In a backhanded way, however, policies that are *not* made can be equally as important since decisions not to interfere with the course of events can have important consequences. In the presence of values that suggest high fertility, nations without a policy of encouraging the adoption of a smaller family standard are decidedly pronatalist.

The key actor in applying population policies is the nation-state. As indicated in Chapter 4, other actors may seek to influence governmental policy, but the initiative for direct action rests with national governments. The targets for their policies are other actors—those couples who, when taken together, have the potential to change the patterns of population activity in response to those policies or in defiance of them. In large part, the success of policy depends upon the extent of agreement between the values of the decision makers, expressed in their programs or directives, and those of the couples who are expected to adjust their behavior in accordance with them. If those couples in the childbearing years can accept a family of a smaller size as their ideal, then government initiatives may be successful. Alternatively, couples may be willing to adapt their values if a government forces a choice betwen increasing family size and higher income through incentives or disincentives. But demographic values are powerful influences and the interplay between policies and those most personal of choices is more sensitive and complicated than agricultural subsidies, housing allowances, and other attempts to influence behavior.

An excellent illustration of the importance of agreement between the population values of a government and those of its citizens can be found in Rumania. That East European nation was faced with sharp declines in fertility after World War II. By 1966 it was reaching a point at which the population would soon cease to reproduce itself and would in fact decline in absolute size. In that year, as the key decision in a set of actions to emphasize pronatalist values, the Rumanian government suddenly eliminated abortion. Since abortion was a major family planning alternative for those couples who sought to limit the size of their families, the result was the intended one. Within a matter of months, the Rumanian birthrate rose sharply, beginning with those women who had already conceived, but who anticipated having an abortion. The birthrate increased from 14.3 in 1966 to 27.4 in 1967. The policy appeared to be successful, but then fertility began to decline once again. Soon, it approached the old levels. The values of the government and those of the Rumanian population did not agree and the population simply found other means to limit fertility. The choice was made despite other disincentives and impediments, including birth premiums, tax increases for unmarried and childless couples over 25, bans on the importation of oral contraceptives, and rewards for mothers with large families.

Efforts to decrease fertility are just as difficult to implement as were those pronatalist attempts of the Rumanian government. Governments do have a variety of weapons available in their policy arsenals. But the choices are conditioned by how coercive they wish to be. The Rumanian case suggests that it may require rather drastic measures to accomplish the goals of forcing increases or decreases in fertility when the values of a culture are essentially supportive of other patterns. The more usual tools involve voluntary efforts based on incentives and disincentives like tax relief or penalties. Chapter 4 provides a full listing of measures from the various nations in which they are employed.

A careful reading of Chapter 4 also offers some insight into the complexities of formulating and applying population policies. It illuminates the way in which policy concerns have become specified since World War II and how the emphasis of those concerns has evolved. Population policy has shifted from attention to the balance between population and resources, especially in Asia, to emerge as an important item in the agenda of global concerns. Equally important, population policy suggests the interplay between academic and political attention to demographic forces, the differing interests of developed and developing nations, those who have different views on the role of population in economic and social development, and private initiatives and governmental policies. Since policy involves the balancing of many different interests, this full discussion suggests the difficulties of dealing crisply with population growth in an atmosphere in which the agenda and the choices for action are still being specified.

FUTURES

A fourth perspective that adds a great deal to the assessment of population problems concerns projections of the future and the various nations that comprise it. Attention to the future is especially important in considering demographic matters because much of the contemporary concern about the pace and scale of population growth involves the reasonable expectation that current rates of increase will continue into the future. The recognition that population growth has a momentum that is difficult to slow because of the possibilities for exponential increases is at the heart of this concern. The past, present, and future represent a unity in assessments of "the population problem" and the debate centers on *when* growth must be curbed. Thus, people talk about "the twenty-ninth day"—the point at which a hypothetical population doubles—as the symbol of the suddenness with which demographic pressures can reach full force.

Because of the close connection of past, present, and future—aided in large part by the fact that population concerns have a strong quantitative dimension—demographers pay special attention to methodological concerns and try to develop reasonable projections of what will happen in the future based upon the trends in the past and present. Chapter 5 suggests how these efforts can proceed when the data are adequate, but, it is hoped, it also suggests that such techniques must be tempered by judgments about human behavior. It is important to reach for clues that discern changes in values and attitudes that may suggest new possibilities in reproductive behavior and other forms of demographic activity.

It is important to emphasize that the future does not yet exist. It will be determined by actors, operating in accordance with basic values and possibly shaped by policy efforts. In this respect, there is a unity to the four perspectives that inform this effort. Demographers are well aware of the interplay among these various components because their predictions about the future are often confounded by sudden shifts in the family size ideals of a population as illustrated by the unexpected baby boom that occurred after World War II or, occasionally, by specific policy initiatives as in Rumania in 1966. Because fertility, mortality, and migration are basic *human* activities, the course of population trends is conditioned by many forces that encourage people to alter their behavior.

But with respect to such matters, one thing is certain. Humankind is now at a turning point. However complicated the assessment of demographic behavior may be or however sophisticated the techniques for estimating the future course of population growth may appear, the conclusion is quite simple. If growth is not checked either by shifts in basic values or by specific, successful policy initiatives, the world faces an unpleasant future. In this sense, however complicated the analysis may need to be for full understanding, "the population problem" is the point at which we both start and end the discussion.

POPULATION TABLE

NO.	REGION AND COUNTRY OR AREA	POPULATION (THOUSANDS)		
		1975	1980	1985
1	WORLD TOTAL	4033183	4414722	4829804
2	MORE DEVELOPED REGIONS	1093182	1130667	1168939
3	LESS DEVELOPED REGIONS	2940002	3284055	3660865
4	A. AFRICA	405847	469361	544545
5	1. EASTERN AFRICA	115291	133551	155665
6	BR. INDIAN OCEAN TERR.	2	2	2
7	BURUNDI	3934	4512	5203
8	COMOROS	300	335	373
9	DJIBOUTI	106	119	135
10	ETHIOPIA	28770	32601	37271
11	KENYA	13531	16402	19864
12	MADAGASCAR	7675	8742	10037
13	MALAWI	5250	6162	7290
14	MAURITIUS (1)	903	995	1086
15	MOZAMBIQUE	9203	10473	12013
16	REUNION	482	525	563
17	RWANDA	4120	4797	5631
18	SEYCHELLES	58	65	72
19	SOMALIA	3170	3645	4214
20	SOUTHERN RHODESIA	6247	7396	8746
21	UGANDA	11337	13201	15478
22	UNITED REP. OF TANZANIA	15393	17934	21057
23	ZAMBIA	4810	5645	6630
24	2. MIDDLE AFRICA	46734	53094	60502
25	ANGOLA	6260	7078	8073
26	CENTRAL AFRICAN EMPIRE	1985	2221	2515
27	CHAD	4030	4524	5124
28	CONGO	1352	1537	1749
29	EQUATORIAL GUINEA	323	363	408
30	GABON	521	551	590
31	SAO TOME AND PRINCIPE	80	85	87
32	UNITED REP. OF CAMEROON	7528	8444	9505
33	ZAIRE	24655	28291	32451
34	3. NORTHERN AFRICA	94071	108731	125480
35	ALGERIA	15680	18594	22215
36	EGYPT	36916	41995	47303
37	LIBYAN ARAB JAMAHIRIYA	2430	2977	3599
38	MOROCCO	17305	20296	23869
39	SUDAN	16015	18371	21153
40	TUNISIA	5608	6363	7186
41	WESTERN SAHARA	117	135	155

146

POPULATION (THOUSANDS)			ANNUAL RATES OF GROWTH (PERCENTAGE)				
1990	1995	2000	75-80	80-85	85-90	90-95	95-20
5275322	5733126	6198638	1.81	1.80	1.76	1.66	1.56
1205832	1239942	1272276	0.67	0.67	0.62	0.56	0.51
4069491	4493183	4926362	2.21	2.17	2.12	1.98	1.84
630373	725624	828052	2.91	2.97	2.93	2.81	2.64
181372	210571	242780	2.94	3.06	3.06	2.99	2.85
2	2	2	0.0	0.0	0.0	0.0	0.0
5991	6869	7832	2.74	2.85	2.82	2.74	2.62
401	425	445	2.21	2.15	1.45	1.16	0.92
152	169	187	2.31	2.52	2.37	2.12	2.02
42639	48707	55347	2.50	2.68	2.69	2.66	2.56
23925	28544	33624	3.85	3.83	3.72	3.53	3.28
11537	13238	15115	2.60	2.76	2.79	2.75	2.65
8628	10179	11928	3.20	3.36	3.37	3.31	3.17
1166	1243	1319	1.94	1.75	1.42	1.28	1.19
13811	15862	18133	2.59	2.74	2.79	2.77	2.68
604	646	686	1.71	1.40	1.41	1.34	1.20
6613	7745	9009	3.04	3.21	3.22	3.16	3.02
80	89	98	2.28	2.05	2.11	2.13	1.93
4843	5525	6260	2.79	2.90	2.78	2.63	2.50
10310	12071	13987	3.38	3.35	3.29	3.15	2.95
18149	21206	24607	3.04	3.18	3.18	3.11	2.97
24757	29020	33794	3.06	3.21	3.24	3.18	3.05
7764	9031	10407	3.20	3.22	3.16	3.02	2.84
68758	77554	86282	2.55	2.61	2.56	2.41	2.13
9233	10522	11874	2.46	2.63	2.69	2.61	2.42
2848	3214	3597	2.25	2.49	2.49	2.42	2.25
5814	6591	7442	2.31	2.49	2.53	2.51	2.43
1984	2231	2468	2.56	2.58	2.52	2.35	2.02
458	511	561	2.34	2.34	2.31	2.19	1.87
639	693	752	1.12	1.37	1.60	1.62	1.63
88	88	88	1.21	0.47	0.23	0.0	0.0
10670	11881	13054	2.30	2.37	2.31	2.15	1.88
37024	41823	46446	2.75	2.74	2.64	2.44	2.10
143982	163557	183667	2.90	2.87	2.75	2.55	2.32
26525	31233	36016	3.41	3.56	3.55	3.27	2.85
52806	58540	64672	2.58	2.38	2.20	2.06	1.99
4289	5025	5768	4.06	3.79	3.51	3.17	2.76
27840	31993	36149	3.19	3.24	3.08	2.78	2.44
24299	27722	31270	2.74	2.82	2.77	2.64	2.41
8045	8841	9563	2.53	2.43	2.26	1.89	1.57
178	203	229	2.82	2.81	2.76	2.59	2.38

(continued)

TABLE 1-A. *(continued)*

NO.	REGION AND COUNTRY OR AREA	POPULATION (THOUSANDS) 1975	1980	1985
42	4. SOUTHERN AFRICA	28767	33012	37628
43	BOTSWANA	716	821	952
44	LESOTHO	1192	1341	1512
45	NAMIBIA	875	1009	1164
46	SOUTH AFRICA	25501	29285	33559
47	SWAZILAND	483	556	641
48	5. WESTERN AFRICA	120984	140973	165070
49	BENIN	3043	3530	4127
50	CAPE VERDE	298	324	351
51	GAMBIA	524	603	666
52	GHANA	9990	11679	13666
53	GUINEA	4416	5014	5700
54	GUINEA-BISSAU	525	573	630
55	IVORY COAST	6710	7973	9290
56	LIBERIA	1574	1863	2193
57	MALI	5807	6646	7648
58	MAURITANIA	1421	1634	1890
59	NIGER	4587	5305	6176
60	NIGERIA	65663	77082	91178
61	ST. HELENA (2)	5	5	6
62	SENEGAL	4977	5661	6474
63	SIERRA LEONE	3045	3474	3997
64	TOGO	2325	2699	3158
65	UPPER VOLTA	6074	6908	7900
66	B. LATIN AMERICA	322592	368476	420603
67	6. CARIBBEAN	27959	30603	33462
68	ANTIGUA	73	75	78
69	BAHAMAS	203	229	257
70	BARBADOS	245	253	263
71	BRITISH VIRGIN ISLANDS	11	13	15
72	CAYMAN ISLANDS	11	12	12
73	CUBA	9340	9978	10654
74	DOMINICA	75	80	85
75	DOMINICAN REPUBLIC	5232	5946	6715
76	GRENADA	96	98	100
77	GUADELOUPE	325	334	346
78	HAITI	5163	5817	6595
79	JAMAICA	2043	2192	2361
80	MARTINIQUE	325	327	335
81	MONTSERRAT	13	13	13
82	NETHERLANDS ANTILLES	241	266	298
83	PUERTO RICO	3113	3438	3724
84	ST. KITTS-NEVIS-ANGUILLA	66	67	67
85	ST. LUCIA	108	115	123
86	ST. VINCENT	93	98	102
87	TRINIDAD AND TOBAGO	1082	1139	1198
88	TURKS AND CAICOS ISLANDS	6	6	6
89	U.S. VIRGIN ISLANDS	95	107	115

POPULATION (THOUSANDS)			ANNUAL RATES OF GROWTH (PERCENTAGE)				
1990	1995	2000	75-80	80-85	85-90	90-95	95-20
42999	48400	53964	2.75	2.72	2.56	2.37	2.18
1101	1272	1439	2.74	2.96	2.91	2.89	2.47
1700	1896	2089	2.36	2.40	2.34	2.18	1.94
1336	1519	1697	2.85	2.86	2.76	2.57	2.22
38125	42875	47803	2.77	2.72	2.55	2.35	2.18
737	838	936	2.82	2.85	2.79	2.57	2.21
193262	225542	261359	3.06	3.16	3.15	3.09	2.95
4828	5632	6529	2.97	3.13	3.14	3.08	2.96
378	403	427	1.67	1.60	1.48	1.28	1.16
783	893	1012	2.81	2.58	2.65	2.63	2.50
15939	18480	21231	3.12	3.14	3.08	2.96	2.78
6471	7318	8214	2.54	2.56	2.54	2.46	2.31
694	766	845	1.75	1.90	1.94	1.97	1.96
10706	12271	13955	3.45	3.06	2.84	2.73	2.57
2574	3000	3464	3.37	3.26	3.20	3.06	2.88
8825	10160	11632	2.70	2.81	2.86	2.82	2.71
2192	2538	2919	2.79	2.91	2.96	2.93	2.80
7208	8391	9670	2.91	3.04	3.09	3.04	2.84
107871	127199	148889	3.21	3.36	3.36	3.30	3.15
6	6	6	0.75	0.73	0.70	0.68	0.66
7425	8501	9682	2.58	2.68	2.74	2.71	2.60
4603	5292	6056	2.64	2.80	2.82	2.79	2.70
3699	4319	5014	2.98	3.14	3.16	3.10	2.98
9060	10373	11814	2.57	2.68	2.74	2.71	2.60
478434	541061	608127	2.66	2.65	2.58	2.46	2.34
36539	39799	43128	1.81	1.79	1.76	1.71	1.61
80	83	85	0.54	0.78	0.51	0.74	0.48
280	303	330	2.41	2.31	1.71	1.58	1.71
274	286	297	0.64	0.78	0.82	0.86	0.75
16	18	19	3.34	2.86	1.29	2.36	1.08
12	13	13	1.74	0.0	0.0	1.60	0.0
11384	12094	12724	1.32	1.31	1.33	1.21	1.02
88	90	91	1.37	1.17	0.83	0.45	0.15
7536	8425	9340	2.56	2.43	2.31	2.23	2.06
102	104	106	0.41	0.40	0.40	0.39	0.38
359	370	381	0.55	0.71	0.74	0.60	0.59
7520	8609	9876	2.39	2.51	2.63	2.70	2.75
2536	2709	2871	1.41	1.49	1.43	1.32	1.16
344	352	359	0.12	0.48	0.53	0.46	0.39
14	14	14	0.0	0.0	1.48	0.0	0.0
330	362	389	1.97	2.27	2.04	1.85	1.44
3976	4203	4406	1.99	1.60	1.31	1.11	0.94
68	69	70	0.30	0.0	0.30	0.29	0.29
127	131	131	1.21	1.31	0.56	0.70	0.0
106	108	110	1.01	0.88	0.65	0.45	0.37
1260	1322	1377	1.03	1.01	1.01	0.96	0.82
6	6	6	0.0	0.0	0.0	0.0	0.0
122	128	133	2.38	1.44	1.18	0.96	0.77

(continued)

TABLE 1-A. *(continued)*

POPULATION (THOUSANDS)

NO.	REGION AND COUNTRY OR AREA	1975	1980	1985
90	7. MIDDLE AMERICA	78857	92806	109235
91	BELIZE	140	162	184
92	COSTA RICA	1965	2213	2485
93	EL SALVADOR	4145	4801	5557
94	GUATEMALA	6243	7262	8403
95	HONDURAS	3095	3693	4374
96	MEXICO	59226	69994	82839
97	NICARAGUA	2322	2737	3223
98	PANAMA	1678	1897	2118
99	CANAL ZONE	43	47	52
100	8. TEMPERATE SOUTH AMERICA	38421	41090	43786
101	ARGENTINA	25377	27056	28669
102	CHILE	10199	11107	12078
103	FALKLAND IS. (MALVINAS)	2	2	2
104	URUGUAY	2843	2925	3037
105	9. TROPICAL SOUTH AMERICA	177354	203977	234119
106	BOLIVIA	4893	5572	6343
107	BRAZIL	109718	126377	145069
108	COLOMBIA	23847	26907	30444
109	ECUADOR	6892	8023	9382
110	FRENCH GUIANA	60	71	82
111	GUYANA	791	884	984
112	PARAGUAY	2651	3067	3546
113	PERU	15485	17773	20361
114	SURINAME	364	389	447
115	VENEZUELA	12653	14914	17461
116	C.10. NORTHERN AMERICA	236379	246350	258494
117	BERMUDA	56	60	64
118	CANADA	22727	24073	25490
119	GREENLAND	50	52	54
120	ST. PIERRE AND MIGUELON	6	6	6
121	UNITED STATES	213540	222159	232880
122	D. EAST ASIA	1063449	1135850	1203638
123	11. CHINA	895339	956848	1014974
124	12. JAPAN	111524	116364	119732
125	13. OTHER EAST ASIA	56586	62638	68932
126	HONG KONG	4367	4801	5240
127	KOREA	50515	55893	61490
128	KOREA, DEM.PEO.REP.OF	15852	17914	20158
129	KOREA, REPUBLIC OF	34663	37979	41332
130	MACAU	260	275	290
131	MONGOLIA	1444	1669	1912

POPULATION (THOUSANDS)			ANNUAL RATES UF GROWTH (PERCENTAGE)				
1990	1995	2000	75-80	80-85	85-90	90-95	95-20
128065	149072	172390	3.26	3.26	3.18	3.04	2.91
205	223	234	2.90	2.53	2.17	1.69	0.95
2776	3075	3377	2.38	2.32	2.21	2.05	1.87
6489	7536	8713	2.94	2.92	3.10	2.99	2.90
9676	11109	12739	3.02	2.92	2.82	2.76	2.74
5107	5955	6981	3.53	3.38	3.10	3.07	3.18
97628	114107	132305	3.34	3.37	3.29	3.12	2.96
3784	4428	5161	3.29	3.27	3.21	3.14	3.06
2347	2585	2825	2.45	2.20	2.05	1.93	1.78
53	54	55	1.81	1.97	0.38	0.41	0.33
46413	48901	51240	1.34	1.27	1.17	1.04	0.93
30180	31573	32850	1.28	1.16	1.03	0.90	0.79
13064	14020	14938	1.71	1.68	1.57	1.41	1.27
2	2	2	0.0	0.0	0.0	0.0	0.0
3167	3306	3450	0.57	0.75	0.84	0.86	0.85
267416	303288	341369	2.80	2.76	2.66	2.52	2.37
7221	8213	9311	2.60	2.59	2.59	2.57	2.51
165743	188258	212491	2.83	2.76	2.66	2.55	2.42
34315	38331	42462	2.41	2.47	2.39	2.21	2.05
10952	12708	14600	3.04	3.13	3.09	2.97	2.78
94	106	118	3.27	3.01	2.70	2.41	2.10
1080	1172	1257	2.22	2.14	1.86	1.64	1.40
4081	4663	5283	2.92	2.90	2.81	2.67	2.50
23214	26266	29468	2.76	2.72	2.62	2.47	2.30
529	617	701	1.33	2.78	3.37	3.08	2.55
20187	22954	25678	3.29	3.15	2.90	2.57	2.24
270469	280878	289546	0.83	0.96	0.91	0.76	0.61
68	72	76	1.38	1.29	1.21	1.14	1.08
26826	27993	29028	1.15	1.14	1.02	0.85	0.73
56	57	58	0.78	0.75	0.73	0.35	0.35
6	6	6	0.0	0.0	0.0	0.0	0.0
243513	252750	260378	0.79	0.94	0.89	0.74	0.59
1274490	1340494	1405916	1.32	1.16	1.14	1.01	0.95
1076373	1133059	1189572	1.33	1.18	1.17	1.03	0.97
122769	125846	128901	0.85	0.57	0.50	0.50	0.48
75348	81589	87443	2.03	1.91	1.78	1.59	1.39
5662	5999	6262	1.89	1.75	1.55	1.16	0.86
67211	72841	78161	2.02	1.91	1.78	1.61	1.41
22549	24969	27371	2.45	2.36	2.24	2.04	1.84
44662	47872	50790	1.83	1.69	1.55	1.39	1.18
305	319	334	1.10	1.05	1.00	0.95	0.90
2170	2430	2686	2.90	2.72	2.53	2.26	2.00

(continued)

TABLE 1-A. *(continued)*

POPULATION (THOUSANDS)

NO.	REGION AND COUNTRY OR AREA	1975	1980	1985
132	E. SOUTH ASIA	1255192	1421712	1606139
133	14. EASTERN SOUTH ASIA	324699	367758	414870
134	BRUNEI	162	191	220
135	BURMA	31240	35289	39858
136	DEMOCRATIC KAMPUCHEA	8110	8872	9810
137	EAST TIMOR	672	755	646
138	INDONESIA (3)	135230	151894	169657
139	LAO PEOPLE'S DEM.REP.	3303	3721	4182
140	MALAYSIA	11983	13640	15412
141	PHILIPPINES	43844	50996	58828
142	SINGAPORE	2250	2427	2614
143	SOC.REP.OF VIET NAM	46546	52299	58707
144	THAILAND	41359	47674	54736
145	15. MIDDLE SOUTH ASIA	845204	955726	1078355
146	AFGHANISTAN	19280	22038	25207
147	BANGLADESH	76582	88705	102833
148	BHUTAN	1160	1298	1453
149	INDIA	618703	693887	775744
150	IRAN	32743	38082	44289
151	MALDIVES	132	148	167
152	NEPAL	12734	14256	15956
153	PAKISTAN	70267	82441	96507
154	SRI LANKA	13603	14871	16199
155	16. WESTERN SOUTH ASIA	85290	98227	112914
156	ARAB COUNTRIES	41133	48280	56601
157	BAHRAIN	256	302	356
158	GAZA STRIP (PALESTINE)	390	438	490
159	IRAQ	11020	13084	15501
160	JORDAN	2702	3190	3764
161	KUWAIT	1002	1372	1770
162	LEBANON	2799	3161	3559
163	OMAN	766	891	1041
164	QATAR	170	220	272
165	SAUDI ARABIA	7180	8367	9784
166	SYRIAN ARAB REPUBLIC	7354	8644	10175
167	UNITED ARAB EMIRATES	558	796	1008
168	YEMEN	5282	5926	6706
169	YEMEN, DEMOCRATIC	1654	1890	2175
170	NON-ARAB COUNTRIES	44157	49947	56313
171	CYPRUS	639	651	670
172	ISRAEL	3455	3950	4418
173	TURKEY	40063	45346	51225

POPULATION (THOUSANDS)			ANNUAL RATES OF GROWTH (PERCENTAGE)				
1990	1995	2000	75-80	80-85	85-90	90-95	95-20
1802590	2004736	2205337	2.49	2.44	2.31	2.13	1.91
464034	512908	559440	2.49	2.41	2.24	2.00	1.74
248	277	306	3.30	2.80	2.40	2.20	2.00
44738	49868	55108	2.44	2.44	2.31	2.17	2.00
10981	12212	13403	1.80	2.01	2.26	2.13	1.86
943	1044	1146	2.33	2.28	2.17	2.03	1.86
187716	205416	221626	2.32	2.21	2.02	1.80	1.52
4678	5199	5725	2.38	2.34	2.24	2.11	1.93
17124	18707	20181	2.59	2.44	2.11	1.77	1.52
67094	75293	83434	3.02	2.86	2.63	2.31	2.05
2803	2963	3095	1.51	1.48	1.40	1.11	0.87
65564	72490	79355	2.33	2.31	2.21	2.01	1.81
62145	69439	76061	2.84	2.76	2.54	2.22	1.82
1209412	1345384	1481801	2.46	2.41	2.29	2.13	1.93
28739	32598	36654	2.67	2.69	2.62	2.52	2.35
118650	135596	153331	2.94	2.96	2.86	2.67	2.46
1632	1827	2036	2.25	2.26	2.32	2.26	2.17
861589	949612	1036664	2.29	2.23	2.10	1.95	1.75
51050	58194	65420	3.02	3.02	2.84	2.62	2.34
188	207	227	2.40	2.40	2.29	2.00	1.80
17921	20110	22432	2.26	2.25	2.32	2.30	2.19
112083	128368	144974	3.20	3.15	2.99	2.71	2.43
17560	18872	20063	1.78	1.71	1.61	1.44	1.22
129144	146444	164097	2.82	2.79	2.69	2.51	2.28
66109	76817	88348	3.20	3.18	3.11	3.00	2.80
416	478	538	3.29	3.32	3.12	2.77	2.37
547	607	671	2.32	2.24	2.20	2.08	2.00
18176	21110	24270	3.43	3.39	3.18	2.99	2.79
4407	5122	5894	3.32	3.31	3.15	3.01	2.81
2194	2672	3166	6.29	5.09	4.29	3.94	3.39
3991	4442	4891	2.43	2.37	2.29	2.14	1.93
1218	1423	1651	3.02	3.11	3.14	3.11	2.97
326	381	434	5.13	4.27	3.63	3.12	2.60
11458	13397	15565	3.06	3.13	3.16	3.13	3.00
11992	14072	16291	3.23	3.26	3.29	3.20	2.93
1215	1425	1635	7.11	4.73	3.73	3.18	2.75
7648	8757	9962	2.30	2.47	2.63	2.71	2.58
2521	2932	3380	2.67	2.81	2.95	3.02	2.85
63035	69627	75749	2.46	2.40	2.26	1.99	1.69
688	701	711	0.37	0.58	0.53	0.37	0.28
4845	5241	5625	2.68	2.24	1.85	1.57	1.41
57502	63685	69413	2.48	2.44	2.31	2.04	1.72

(continued)

TABLE 1-A. *(continued)*   POPULATION (THOUSANDS)

NO.	REGION AND COUNTRY OR AREA	1975	1980	1985
174	F. EUROPE	474172	483532	492395
175	17. EASTERN EUROPE	106182	110041	113538
176	BULGARIA	8722	9007	9237
177	CZECHOSLUVAKIA	14802	15336	15794
178	GERMAN DEM. REP. (4)	16850	16864	16877
179	HUNGARY	10541	10761	10919
180	POLAND	34022	35805	37558
181	ROMANIA	21245	22268	23153
182	18. NORTHERN EUROPE	81580	81925	82215
183	CHANNEL ISLANDS	128	133	138
184	DENMARK	5060	5105	5137
185	FAEROE ISLANDS	40	41	43
186	FINLAND	4711	4818	4907
187	ICELAND	218	231	243
188	IRELAND	3127	3307	3484
189	ISLE OF MAN	61	65	68
190	NORWAY	4007	4075	4143
191	SWEDEN	8193	8262	8295
192	UNITED KINGDOM	56035	55888	55757
193	19. SOUTHERN EUROPE	134080	139010	143682
194	ANDORRA	27	31	35
195	ALBANIA	2424	2734	3053
196	GIBRALTAR	30	33	35
197	GREECE	9047	9329	9609
198	HOLY SEE	1	1	1
199	ITALY	55830	56959	58030
200	MALTA	328	340	353
201	PORTUGAL	9425	9856	10282
202	SAN MARINO	20	21	22
203	SPAIN	35596	37378	38999
204	YUGOSLAVIA	21352	22328	23263
205	20. WESTERN EUROPE	152330	152556	152960
206	AUSTRIA	7520	7481	7463
207	BELGIUM	9796	9920	10076
208	FRANCE	52707	53450	54265
209	GERMANY, FED.REP. OF (4)	61832	60903	60013
210	LIECHTENSTEIN	24	26	28
211	LUXEMBOURG	357	358	358
212	MONACO	25	26	27
213	NETHERLANDS	13664	14082	14446
214	SWITZERLAND	6405	6310	6284

POPULATION (THOUSANDS)			ANNUAL RATES OF GROWTH (PERCENTAGE)				
1990	1995	2000	75-80	80-85	85-90	90-95	95-20
501170	510436	520223	0.39	0.36	0.35	0.37	0.38
116479	119136	121846	0.71	0.63	0.51	0.45	0.45
9413	9558	9698	0.64	0.50	0.38	0.31	0.29
16233	16683	17196	0.71	0.59	0.55	0.55	0.61
16852	16789	16748	0.02	0.02	-0.03	-0.07	-0.05
11020	11117	11259	0.41	0.29	0.18	0.18	0.25
38967	40119	41217	1.02	0.96	0.74	0.58	0.54
23994	24870	25728	0.94	0.78	0.71	0.72	0.68
82756	83608	84546	0.08	0.07	0.13	0.20	0.22
143	147	152	0.77	0.74	0.71	0.55	0.67
5174	5228	5291	0.18	0.12	0.14	0.21	0.24
44	45	47	0.49	0.95	0.46	0.45	0.87
4981	5047	5112	0.45	0.37	0.30	0.26	0.26
254	266	277	1.16	1.01	0.89	0.92	0.81
3661	3837	4009	1.12	1.04	0.99	0.94	0.88
70	71	72	1.27	0.90	0.58	0.28	0.28
4224	4312	4405	0.34	0.33	0.39	0.41	0.43
8329	8398	8507	0.17	0.08	0.08	0.17	0.26
55876	56257	56674	-0.05	-0.05	0.04	0.14	0.15
148112	152321	156280	0.72	0.66	0.61	0.56	0.51
38	39	40	3.18	2.22	1.52	0.95	0.46
3363	3652	3912	2.41	2.21	1.93	1.65	1.38
36	37	38	1.91	1.18	0.56	0.55	0.53
9886	10149	10395	0.61	0.59	0.57	0.53	0.48
1	1	1	0.0	0.0	0.0	0.0	0.0
59048	60053	61016	0.40	0.37	0.35	0.34	0.32
366	377	387	0.72	0.75	0.72	0.59	0.52
10694	11088	11466	0.89	0.85	0.79	0.72	0.67
23	24	25	0.98	0.93	0.89	0.85	0.82
40541	42005	43362	0.98	0.85	0.78	0.71	0.64
24116	24896	25638	0.89	0.82	0.72	0.64	0.59
153823	155371	157551	0.03	0.05	0.11	0.20	0.28
7475	7523	7612	-0.10	-0.05	0.03	0.13	0.24
10288	10513	10762	0.25	0.31	0.42	0.43	0.47
55182	56147	57281	0.28	0.30	0.34	0.35	0.40
59405	59283	59546	-0.30	-0.29	-0.20	-0.04	0.09
30	32	33	1.60	1.48	1.38	1.29	0.62
358	359	361	0.06	0.0	0.0	0.06	0.11
28	29	30	0.78	0.75	0.73	0.70	0.68
14741	15113	15487	0.60	0.51	0.40	0.50	0.49
6316	6372	6439	-0.30	-0.08	0.10	0.18	0.21

(continued)

TABLE 1-A. *(continued)*   POPULATION (THOUSANDS)

NO.	REGION AND COUNTRY OR AREA	1975	1980	1985
215	G. OCEANIA	21159	22775	24433
216	21. AUSTRALIA-NEW ZEALAND	16714	17755	18760
217	AUSTRALIA	13627	14487	15300
218	NEW ZEALAND	3087	3268	3460
219	22. MELANESIA	3132	3568	4075
220	NEW CALEDONIA	131	154	183
221	NEW HEBRIDES	96	109	121
222	NORFOLK ISLAND	2	2	2
223	PAPUA NEW GUINEA	2716	3082	3511
224	SOLOMON ISLANDS	189	221	258
225	23. MICRONESIA-POLYNESIA	1313	1452	1597
226	MICRONESIA (8)	307	354	405
227	GILBERT ISLANDS	59	66	73
228	GUAM	104	120	141
229	NAURU	8	8	9
230	NIUE	5	6	6
231	PACIFIC ISLANDS	121	143	165
232	TUVALU	0	0	0
233	OTHER MICRONESIA (5)	10	11	12
234	POLYNESIA	1005	1099	1192
235	AMERICAN SAMOA	29	31	33
236	COOK ISLANDS	25	27	30
237	FIJI	570	619	665
238	FRENCH POLYNESIA	133	155	181
239	SAMOA	150	161	172
240	TONGA	90	96	102
241	WALLIS AND FUTUNA IS.	9	9	9
242	H.24. U.S.S.R.	254393	266666	279558

NOTES --

(1) INCLUDING AGALEGA, RODRIGUES, AND ST. BRANDON.
(2) INCLUDING ASCENSION AND TRISTAN DA CUNHA.
(3) INCLUDING WEST IRIAN.
(4) THE DATA WHICH RELATE TO THE FEDERAL REPUBLIC OF GERMANY AND
     THE GERMAN DEMOCRATIC REPUBLIC INCLUDE THE RELEVANT DATA
     RELATING TO BERLIN FOR WHICH SEPARATE DATA HAVE NOT BEEN
     SUPPLIED. THIS IS WITHOUT PREJUDICE TO ANY QUESTION OF STATUS
     WHICH MAY BE INVOLVED.
(5) INCLUDING CANTON AND ENDERBURY ISLANDS, CHRISTMAS ISLAND,
     COCOS (KEELING) ISLANDS, JOHNSTON ISLAND, MIDWAY ISLANDS,
     PITCAIRN ISLAND, TOKELAU AND WAKE ISLAND.

POPULATION (THOUSANDS)			ANNUAL RATES OF GROWTH (PERCENTAGE)				
1990	1995	2000	75-80	80-85	85-90	90-95	95-20
26161	27915	29620	1.47	1.41	1.37	1.30	1.19
19787	20801	21789	1.21	1.10	1.07	1.00	0.93
16133	16955	17762	1.22	1.09	1.06	0.99	0.93
3654	3846	4027	1.14	1.14	1.09	1.02	0.92
4633	5237	5836	2.60	2.66	2.56	2.45	2.16
215	249	282	3.35	3.43	3.16	3.01	2.48
136	151	166	2.58	2.20	2.22	2.17	1.83
2	2	2	0.0	0.0	0.0	0.0	0.0
3979	4486	4986	2.53	2.61	2.50	2.40	2.11
302	349	400	3.15	3.12	3.13	2.91	2.74
1741	1876	1995	2.02	1.90	1.72	1.50	1.22
460	517	575	2.80	2.72	2.53	2.34	2.12
80	88	95	1.99	2.06	1.99	1.74	1.58
163	187	213	2.94	3.10	2.97	2.77	2.58
9	10	10	1.29	1.21	1.14	1.08	1.03
7	7	7	1.43	1.33	1.25	1.18	1.11
188	211	234	3.30	2.90	2.57	2.36	2.05
0	0	0	0.0	0.0	0.0	0.0	0.0
13	14	16	1.68	1.74	1.69	1.60	1.60
1281	1360	1420	1.78	1.63	1.44	1.19	0.87
35	37	39	1.34	1.25	1.18	1.11	1.05
33	36	37	2.31	2.07	1.58	1.46	1.10
706	740	764	1.65	1.43	1.20	0.94	0.64
207	231	247	3.17	3.03	2.73	2.19	1.31
183	194	205	1.36	1.32	1.24	1.17	1.10
108	113	119	1.29	1.21	1.14	0.90	1.04
9	9	9	0.0	0.0	0.0	0.0	0.0
291637	301981	311817	0.94	0.94	0.85	0.70	0.64

Source:

World Population Trends and Prospects, By Country, 1950-2000: Summary Report of the 1978 Assessment (New York: Department of International Economic and Social Affairs, United Nations, 1979), Table 1-A, pp. 15-20, ST/ESA/SER.R/33.

ANNOTATED BIBLIOGRAPHY

POPULATION AS A GLOBAL ISSUE

There are a number of sources that provide an excellent introduction to the evolution and/or the basic characteristics of the population problem. One such source is Thomas Robert Malthus, *An Essay on Population*, (New York: Augustus Kelley, Booksellers, 1798; reprinted, 1965). This is the classic statement of the relationship between population growth and resources. The essay should be required reading for all who are interested in population issues, not only for its historical value, but for its contribution to the commonly held understandings of population issues.

A basic introduction to population concerns and the methods for their analysis is John R. Weeks, *Population: An Introduction to Concepts and Issues*, (Belmont, Calif.: Wadsworth Publishers, 1981, Second Edition). Week's text is only one of many such choices, but it is noteworthy for its coverage, currentness, clarity of presentation, and balance.

A third source addresses population issues other than rapid growth, John Berger's *A Seventh Man: Migrant Workers in Europe*, (New York: The Viking Press, 1975). In Europe, an important issue is the decline of population and the need to "import" workers to provide the needed manpower. Berger looks at the 12 million workers, mainly from "developing" nations, who have made the move to European cities for better employment opportunities. But, as he observes with dramatic support from Jean Mohr's photography, "to be homeless is to be nameless" and the migrants face loneliness, statelessness, and humilitation.

A fourth source, Neil W. Chamberlain's *Beyond Malthus: Population and Power*, (New York: Basic Books, 1970, reacts to the emphasis in considerations of the "population explosion" as a population/resource question. Rather, he argues that the major impact is a matter of the shape in political and economic power within and between societies. Population pressures redistribute power, privilege, and income to the advantage of a few and the disadvantage of many.

158

A book questioning the conventional wisdom about population issues is a collection of articles by Howard M. Bahr, Bruce A. Chadwick, and Darwin L. Thomas: *Population, Resources, and the Future: Non-Malthusian Perspectives*, (Provo, Utah: Brigham Young Press, 1972). It questions the attack on families with more than two children and raises the possibility that "accepting population size as the critical causal variable brings premature closure on the causal relationships in a very complex system."

Richard A. Easterlin, an economic demographer, examines the way in which the relative size of an individual's generation (or cohort) determines the individual's opportunities and fortunes. *Birth and Fortune: The Impact of Numbers on Personal Welfare*, (New York: Basic Books, 1980) focuses upon prospects within the American society and economy, but it raises a set of important demographic issues that apply worldwide, especially when the size of the cohorts change dramatically.

Finally, a pamphlet outlining the Marxist perspective on population matters is Joseph Hansen's *The "Population Explosion": How Socialists View It*, Second Edition, (New York: The Pathfinder Press, 1970). It is polemical in tone and analysis, but it offers a clear alternative to the Malthusian interpretation of the consequences of demographic growth. Since such approaches to political philosophy shape the policies of many nations, the socialist explanation is of more than passing interest.

ACTORS AND VALUES

Much of the literature analyzing population actors and values is several years old. Of the works published since 1974 and the World Population Conference Nicholas J. Demerath, *Birth Control and Foreign Policy: The Alternatives to Family Planning* (New York: Harper & Row, Publishers, 1976) is perhaps the most useful, especially since it is available in paperback. Although written in a somewhat polemical tone, this book compares the family planning approach to other alternatives, most importantly what the author calls the "societal" approach to fertility control. In doing so, it traces the evolution of the worldwide family planning network. Unfortunately the comparison of India and China, as leading examples of the two contending approaches, is quite dated, given the recent flood of information on China.

Two other books dealing with population actors and values are Terry L. McCoy (ed.), *The Dynamics of Population Policy in Latin America* (Cambridge, Mass: Ballinger Publishing Company, 1974) and Phyllis Tilson Piotrow, *World Population Crises* (New York: Prager Publishers, 1973). Although both were published prior to the World Population Conference at Bucharest, they do deal explicitly with global actors and other values. As for the Conference itself, a meeting of direct encounter among the various actors and value positions, an excellent treatment is found in W. Parker Marden, *et al.*, "A Report on Bucharest" *Studies in Family Planning*, 5, No. 12 (December 1974).

Perhaps the most valuable literature on population actors and values are the materials published by the actors themselves. Virtually all produce at least an annual report while many, such as IPPF and the Population Reference Bureau, publish periodic newsletters that carry population news in general and statements of the organizations activities and evolving value position in particular. Even UNFPA and the U.S. Department of State produce rather substantial documentary evidence of their projects and positions. The most comprehensive and objective publication effort is that of the Population Council. It includes the research paper series *Studies in Family Planning* and the quarterly journal *Population and Development Review*. Information about Council publications can be obtained from: Publications Office, The Population Council, One Dag Hammar-Skjold Plaza, New York, NY 10017.

POLICY

The best source for current information concerning the fertility reduction policies and programs of Third World countries is Dorothy L. Nortman and Ellen Hofstatters's *Population and Family Planning Programs,* 10th edition (New York: The Population Council, 1980). This ninety-four page "factbook" contains eighty pages of tables enumerating not only government fertility reduction policies and programs but also measures of "input" to and "output" from specific countries' fertility reduction programs. Here you can find such "input" measures as government expenditures for family planning programs and the size of program staffs. You can find "output" measures such as the number of "acceptors" in government programs and estimates of the percentage of the population using contraceptives. Although you will not find much commentary about the content of the twenty-four tables making up the factbook, the wealth of information contained in the tables as well as their clear presentation make this a first stop for anyone wishing to become acquainted with current Third World governmental efforts to reduce fertility.

A good source for a broader treatment of contemporary government population policies is *World Population Trends and Policies: 1977 Monitoring Report, Vol. II, Population Policies* (New York: United Nations, 1979; sales number E. 78. XIII.4). The primary source for the information in the volume is a 1976 United Nation's survey which was answered by two-thirds of member states. Here you will find information not just on the population policies of Third World countries but also of developed countries. Migration and mortality policies are treated as well as fertility policy. Unlike in the Nortman and Hofstatter volume pronatalist as well as fertility reduction positions are given explicit treatment.

All the documents which were prepared for the World Population Conference held at Bucharest, Romania, in 1974 are to be found in *The Population Debate: Dimensions and Perspectives,* Vols I and II (New York: United Nations, 1975; sales numbers E/F/S. 75. XIII. 4 and E/F/S. 75 XIII.5). The text of the World Population Plan of Action adopted by the Conference is to be found in Vol. 1. The fourteen hundred pages of articles are generally authored by experts within the field and treat the full spectrum of population related topics. A selective reading of various articles can familiarize the reader with the "debate" which exists within demography and economics concerning the nature of contemporary "population" problems.

World Population Policies (New York: Praeger, 1979) edited by Jyoti Shankar Singh provides coverage of post-Bucharest developments. This volume contains not only a reprint of the World Population Plan of Action but also a brief summary of the recommendations coming from the five "regional consultations" which took place after Bucharest. There is also a condensed version of a U.N. monitoring report on population policies (item 2 of the bibliography) and the monitoring report on population trends (see item 2 of the bibliography following Chapter 4), as well as a treatment of recent trends (1970−77) in international population assistance and a description of the current and planned activities of the United Nations Fund for Population Activities.

FUTURES

The U.N. Population projections examined in this chapter are from the *Summary Report of the 1978 Assessment*, a document which is basically just tables with little commentary, analysis, or discussion of assumptions and methodology. Until the public version of the 1978 assessment is readied, those interested in learning more about the U.N. approach to population projection can find a description of basic methods, assumptions, and sources of data used in U.S. projections in *World Population Prospects as Assessed in 1973* (New York: United Nations, 1977; sales publication number E. 76. XIII. 4).

A very comprehensive analysis of world-wide population trends of the recent past (since 1950) and their implications for the future is to be found in *World Population Trends and Policies: 1977 Monitoring Report, Vol 1, Population Trends* (New York: United Nations, 1979, sales number E. 78. XIII. 3). This volume contains analysis and discussion of the following trends: world and regional population size and growth rates; mortality; fertility; age distribution; sex composition; migration; labor force; urbanization; education; and food.

Illustrative Projections of World Populations to the 21st Century, No. 79 of the Special Studies Series P-23 of the U.S. Bureau of the Census' *Current Population Reports* (Washington: Department of Commerce, 1979) contains a brief and clear description of the assumptions and methods employed by the Census Bureau in making its projections. A comparison of these assumptions and the projections they produce with those of the U.S. examined in this chapter will illustrate how different demographers, examining the same past trends and using a similar methodology, can arrive at somewhat different projections of the future.

A good brief description of the "cohort component" method of population projection can be found in Chapter 15 of the *The Global 2000 Report to the President, Vol II: The Technical Report* (Washington: Government Printing Office, 1980). Both the U.N. and the U.S. Census demographers use the "cohort component" method. This chapter describes this method and also examines some of the assumptions underlying the Census projections and the projections of the Community and Family Study Center of the University of Chicago. Chapter 2 of this volume contains the world population projections of these two groups.

INDEX

THE EDITORS

James E. Harf is professor of political science and a Mershon Senior Faculty, The Ohio State University. In addition to a volume in the Global Issues Series, he is coauthor of *International and Comparative Politics: A Handbook* and coeditor of *Strategy Security and Policy: National and Global Dimensions.* He is executive director of the Consortium for International Studies Education and serves as a consultant on international and global studies education at a number of universities and colleges. He is coeditor of the Global Issues Series, Learning Materials in National Security Education Series and Learning Materials in International Studies Series. Previously he was a visiting professor at Duke University.

B. Thomas Trout is an associate professor of political science at the University of New Hampshire. He has his undergraduate degree from UCLA and his Ph.D. and a Russia Area Certificate from Indiana University. He is the chairman of Consortium for International Studies Education, a member of the Executive Council of the section for military studies of the International Studies Association and a member of the governing council of the latter organization. Professor Trout consults to a number of programs in International Education and has spoken extensively on the need for a Global Issues perspective on international affairs. He is a contributor and coeditor of *Understanding Global Issues,* a framework for Analysis and Strategy, Security and Policy: National and International Dimensions. He is also co-editor of the *Global Issues Series, Learning Materials in National Security Education* and has published articles in the *American Political Science Review, International Studies Quarterly, Naval War College Review,* and other scholarly journals.

THE CONTRIBUTING AUTHORS

Terry L. McCoy is associate director of the Center for Latin American Studies and associate professor of Latin American studies, political science, and sociology at the University of Florida. His work on population policies and international migration has been supported by grants from the Population Council and National Institutes of Health. He is editor of *The Dynamics of Population Policy in Latin America* (Ballinger, 1974) and the author of numerous papers on population growth and distribution policies.

Parker G. Marden is the Charles A. Dana Professor of Sociology at St. Lawrence University, Canton, New York. He received his A.B. from Bates College and an A.M. and Ph.D. from Brown University. He has also taught at Cornell and Lawrence Universities. His interests in social demography were shaped by six years in the International Population Program at Cornell where he conducted research in Honduras, Colombia, and Belize. He is coeditor with Dennis Hodgson of *Population, Environment, and the Quality of Life.*

Dennis Hodgson is an assistant professor of sociology at Fairfield University. He received his Ph.D. from the International Population Program of Cornell University. His doctoral and latter research has focused on demographic theory and policy. He is coeditor with Parker Marden of *Population, Environment, and the Quality of Life*.